# TOWARDS A NEW PENSIONS SETTLEMENT

# About Policy Network

Policy Network is an international thinktank and research institute. Its network spans national borders across Europe and the wider world with the aim of promoting the best progressive thinking on the major social and economic challenges of the 21st century.

Our work is driven by a network of politicians, policymakers, business leaders, public service professionals, and academic researchers who work on long-term issues relating to public policy, political economy, social attitudes, governance and international affairs. This is complemented by the expertise and research excellence of Policy Network's international team.

A platform for research and ideas

- Promoting expert ideas and political analysis on the key economic, social and political challenges of our age.
- Disseminating research excellence and relevant knowledge to a wider public audience through interactive policy networks, including interdisciplinary and scholarly collaboration.
- Engaging and informing the public debate about the future of European and global progressive politics.

A network of leaders, policymakers and thinkers

- Building international policy communities comprising individuals and affiliate institutions.
- Providing meeting platforms where the politically active, and potential leaders of the future, can engage with each other across national borders and with the best thinkers who are sympathetic to their broad aims.
- Engaging in external collaboration with partners including higher education institutions, the private sector, thinktanks, charities, community organisations, and trade unions.
- Delivering an innovative events programme combining in-house seminars with large-scale public conferences designed to influence and contribute to key public debates.

www.policy-network.net

# TOWARDS A NEW PENSIONS SETTLEMENT

## *The International Experience*

## Volume III

### Edited by
### Gregg McClymont, Andy Tarrant
### and Tim Gosling

the
**people's**
pension

}{

policy network

ROWMAN &
LITTLEFIELD
———— INTERNATIONAL ————

London • New York

Published by Rowman & Littlefield International Ltd.
Unit A, Whitacre, 26-34 Stannary Street, London, SE11 4AB
www.rowmaninternational.com

Rowman & Littlefield International Ltd. is an affiliate of Rowman & Littlefield
4501 Forbes Boulevard, Suite 200, Lanham, Maryland 20706, USA
With additional offices in Boulder, New York, Toronto (Canada), and
Plymouth (UK)
www.rowman.com

**British Library Cataloguing in Publication Data**

A catalogue record for this book is available from the British Library

ISBN: PB 978-1-78661-285-4
ISBN: eBook 978-1-78661-286-1

**Library of Congress Cataloging-in-Publication Data**

Library of Congress Control Number: 2017958878

∞™ The paper used in this publication meets the minimum requirements of
American National Standard for Information Sciences—Permanence of Paper for
Printed Library Materials, ANSI/NISO Z39.48-1992.

# CONTENTS

# ACKNOWLEDGEMENTS

We would like to thank the contributing authors. We would also like to thank all those who discussed the issues raised in the chapters with us and in particular staff at B&CE, provider of The People's Pension.

# INTRODUCTION: PENSION SYSTEMS FIT FOR PENSIONERS

## The international experience

## Gregg McClymont, Andy Tarrant and Tim Gosling

**2**018's *Towards a new pension settlement: The international experience*, volume II, looked at the strengths and weaknesses of pension systems which were early adopters of defined contribution (DC). Our third volume continues this comparative approach, this time including a particular focus on how successfully national pension systems deliver a retirement income on a reasonable proportion of pre-retirement wages. While delivering a stable income in retirement ought to be the primary focus of a workplace pension system, this is not the case in most Anglo-Saxon countries, including the UK. The focus in these countries has been on the accumulation of a fund rather than on the quality of the national system in turning that fund into a reliable source of retirement income. Where a country is introduced for the first time in these volumes, the author sets out the wider characteristics of the pension system in order to explain the context in which sits the retirement regime of the country.

## THE COUNTRIES INCLUDED IN THIS VOLUME

This volume considers the pension systems in Canada, Chile, Denmark, France, Germany, Greece, Indonesia and Switzerland. We also include a chapter on the introduction of collective defined contribution (CDC) pensions in the UK, which is an example of pension policy learning from international experience. CDC dominates the Dutch pension system (discussed in volume I), it has been adopted in some Canadian provinces (also discussed in volume I), and is, some might argue, characteristic of many Danish funds (discussed below). As the chapter on Germany (also previously discussed in volume I) suggests, CDC is likely to be adopted as the main form of workplace pension in the Federal Republic too.

The Chile and Denmark chapters focus on retirement, while the Canadian chapter ranges more widely, providing the background for the CDC reform in New Brunswick that was covered in our first volume. Chile is particularly interesting from a UK perspective since Chilean retirees get better value for money when they purchase an annuity than British purchasers do. Chile has an independent national brokerage system, which ensures that potential annuitants are offered the best available annuity. Chile has been able to harness the market to work in the annuitant's interest. This stands in contrast with the UK where less effective information 'remedies' continue to be preferred by the regulator of retail annuities – the Financial Conduct Authority ("FCA") – despite the regulator's own research suggesting that the proposed information remedy will lead the vast majority of potential annuitants to continue to default, that is 'rollover' into the annuity offered by their savings provider – even when this provides poorer value than alternative offerings that could be found by 'shopping around'[1].

The countries examined for the first time in this volume are France, Greece, Indonesia and Switzerland. France and Switzerland are ideal-type examples of a state-run pay-as-you-go (PAYG) system and a fiduciary-based system respectively. Each of these systems generate income effectively and efficiently for current retirees but are subject to pressures for accrual reform in order to remain sustainable. The Macron presidency is seeking to develop DC workplace pensions, and this is also a direction of travel in Greece. Indonesia, on the other hand, is building a state provided workplace defined benefit ("DB") pension system, existing DC arrangements having proven unsatisfactory from an income point of view. Canada's second pillar system is efficient, but coverage is patchy and efforts are underway to expand its reach.

From our analysis, some universal themes emerge from the chapters in this volume as the basis for a successful pension system:

- Comprehensive coverage of the population
- Reasonable levels of contributions
- Fiduciary governance with scale as the means to ensuring reasonable costs and charges
- Transparency of costs
- The organisation of the pension system so as to deliver income in retirement
- Longevity protection

## DC RETIREMENT IN THE UK

In the UK, the issue of retirement income is a live one. There is an emerging difference between those who see pensions as long-term savings products that can be used as the employee sees fit and might be used, as one option, to buy an income in a marketplace and those who see pensions as fundamentally about preparing and providing a retirement income across the life course. The UK 'disruptors', that is, the new pension funds – master trusts – that provide auto-enrolment pensions at low cost to those on low and middle incomes, are likely to mimic some of the best international practice to provide a 'whole of life' pension product. Their success will depend in part on recognition by policy makers of the stark differences between retail pensions and pension providers under trust law i.e. a fiduciary duty. One of the key distinguishing points between systems is the presence of a trustee that acts as a surrogate informed customer on the part of members.

The master trusts are being mandated by their trustees to develop retirement products by combining income drawdown and annuity. The annuities will be bulk-bought from the wider market and the best wholesale price passed on to members, thereby mimicking on a scheme level what Chile has introduced on a national basis, as we shall see. The merit of the annuity element of the retirement product is that it ensures members have longevity protection so that they cannot run out of money in later life. Members in these schemes would be put on a glidepath towards these retirement income products in such a way that taking a retirement income could be achieved without leaving the fund.

This trust-based approach stands in contrasts to the state of play in the UK's other type of workplace pension, namely retail contract-based schemes, which, are subject to weaker governance arrangements and a system of rules based on conduct regulation, not fiduciary duties.

## GOVERNANCE OF PENSIONS IN THE UK

The UK is quite unusual in allowing employers to have the option to choose, on behalf of their employees, a provider which does not have a legal duty to prioritise their interests, and where the provider is a private market operator. This is not the case in Australia, Greece, Ireland (although there are exceptions), Mexico, Netherlands, New Zealand, Switzerland and the United States. In other northern European countries, like Denmark and Germany, trade unions are on the board of the pension scheme. In France, Greece, Indonesia and Italy, the state is the primary provider.

The risk of allowing private providers to behave as if pensions are a normal market but where normal demand side constraints do not apply, is that they will charge excessive prices on a sustained basis and provide products whose supply suits them but may not be well-adapted to consumer needs. Demand side constraints on supplier quality are weak because selection is not conducted by employees, who instead receive a 'take-it-or-leave-it' offer from the employer. An employer, particularly a smaller, less-resourced employer – which in reality is the vast majority of cases – is unlikely to be willing or able to do anything should a pensions product be revealed as inferior forty years down the line, and in many instances, these companies will no longer exist. With the rate of job churn, the directly affected individual is highly likely to be a former employee in any case.

Nor is the individual saver – even if they were the buyer – in a stronger position to ensure value for money. A host of well-known behavioural biases captured in the work of behavioural economists, including present bias and inertia, have a negative impact on buyer behaviour[2]. As do vast – unbridgeable – information asymmetries. As mentioned above, the UK regulator's research on responses to price-signals on annuities found that a large majority of people ignored them. The FCA's subsequent research into the wider retirement product market also underlines that large numbers of consumers are not acting as informed rational purchasers[3].

This is why governance matters so much when it comes to pensions. UK trust-based providers are legally obliged to put members' interests first. This is not the case for the UK's contract-based retail providers. The 2013 report of the Office of Fair Trading (OFT) into UK DC pensions identified the problem of conflicted interests and poor governance in retail pensions leading to poor outcomes. The OFT recommendation that policy should be used to promote "robust independent governance" eventually resulted in the establishment of Independent Governance Committees ("IGCs")[4]. This model is a flawed first attempt at delivering "robust independent governance". Notably, the IGCs are not necessarily required to be entirely independent nor are they truly 'governing' either.

Retail providers are obliged to treat members "fairly". This is an ambiguous term. It is also a principle that is not justiciable by courts on behalf of consumers but is enforced (or not, as the case may be) by the FCA. In practice, none of the major reforms of workplace pensions in the last five years have been initiated by the FCA applying its principles. Instead, they have required legislative intervention driven forward by political pressures and the policy objectives of government. EU law has made a nominal change, obliging the FCA to include a requirement in its principles for providers to act in the best interests of the "client", which might potentially be actionable in the courts. However, it is not currently being interpreted as a fiduciary duty. In the United States, advisers to whom regulators wanted to attach a fiduciary duty have lobbied instead for a 'client's best interest standard'. The view appears to be that a 'client's best interests' can more easily be met by the provision of information, whereas a "beneficiary's" interest requires the provider to be more proactive.

## INDEPENDENT GOVERNANCE COMMITTEES

In a master trust or single employer trust, trustees are responsible in law for the running of the scheme. In a master trust pension scheme, it is the trustees that have to apply for authorisation to The Pensions Regulator (which regulates trust-based pensions). Trustees of larger schemes operate in a manner similar to board members in a publicly listed company (PLC). Those familiar with PLC board members will know that shareholder value is a constant concern. Replacing the term "shareholder" with "member" provides a feel for how such trustees operate. The trustees can sack the underlying provider if they deem it to be no longer meeting the members' best interest. The requirements on trustees to avoid conflicts of interest are strict.

IGCs do not have the same legal powers as trustees. They have an advisory rather than an executive role. While in theory they could complain to the FCA if their views are ignored, this power is far weaker than that of trustees. The contract provider is also permitted to appoint a minority of members to the IGC, who are not independent. The latter are thereby able to monitor the behaviour of the independent members on behalf of the firm and they can vote on decisions. In addition, those appointees that meet the definition of independence include employees of other companies providing services to the contract-based provider, as long as Chinese walls are appropriately managed. This reveals a highly optimistic expectation on the part of the regulator that behavioural rules will overcome structural incentives. The FCA has shelved the review of IGC's effectiveness which was promised previously, while proceeding with plans to extend their remit to the decumulation phase.

The FCAs current strategy for ensuring good outcomes in the retail environment entails ensuring consumers

1. can no longer be defaulted into cash when they buy an income drawdown product;
2. must select from a series of investment pathways depending on risk appetite; and
3. extends the advisory role of Independent Government Committees (IGCs) to cover retirement products.

It is unlikely to succeed given the weakness in the retail space of consumer protections, the reality of consumer behavioural biases, and the sheer size of information asymmetries.

## COLLECTIVE DEFINED CONTRIBUTION (CDC) SCHEMES

CDC has attracted interest because it can remove the need for a pension scheme to go to the market to buy annuities for members at retirement. This would reduce some of the costs involved in annuitisation – although it is unlikely to make a large difference to the size of retirement incomes on average. CDC schemes can however potentially reduce volatility in member outcomes. Annuitisation involves a one-off decision at a single point in time, thus the individual carries heavy market risk. CDC reduces this particular risk. The individual may still potentially face a drop in expected income in a particular year, but since total assets have not been crystallised, the individual's assets will be revalued as markets recover and greater income may be received again in future years. CDC schemes may or may not include buffer funds which serve to prevent falls in income altogether (but which also absorb some or all of greater than expected returns to replenish the buffer). Buffer funds and other forms of intergenerational smoothing are more controversial since they are forms of cross-subsidy that may or may not be fairly distributed across generations. The UK government is interested in CDC, but without buffers.

Our Danish expert takes the view that Danish workplace pensions are not CDC because they (mostly) no longer provided guarantees. However, looking at it from the UK perspective, Danish workplace pensions look like CDC because members own investment units in accumulation and in retirement, and the annuities provided by these schemes fluctuate in value depending on market circumstances. This is very close, in UK terms, to being categorised as a money purchase benefit. However, the Danish retirement products are collective in nature as the assets are pooled and longevity protection applies. The globally renowned Dutch workplace CDC pension system – as we discuss in volume I – could end up in a similar place, albeit coming from a DB background.

## STATE PENSION

Pension systems are usually understood through the World Bank typology of three pillars: state pensions, employer-based workplace pensions, and voluntary individual pension products. In most countries, the vast majority of the population has pensions in the first pillar only. As a working hypothesis, a neutral observer might think that the greater the amount of income provided by the state pension in retirement, the less one would have to be concerned about the efficiency of the workplace pension system. Bearing this in mind, our neutral observer might also spot that the UK has one of the least generous

Table 1.1    Comparison of Replacement Rates of Average Wage in Retirement

| Country | Replacement rate pre-tax of state pension | Replacement rate pre-tax of state pension and mandatory or semi-mandatory workplace pension | Replacement rate post-tax of state pension and mandatory or semi-compulsory workplace pension |
|---|---|---|---|
| UK | 22% | 40% | 47% |
| Canada | 41% | 41% | 53.4% |
| Chile | 0% | 33.5% | 40% |
| Denmark* | 39.5%** | 36.5% | 80.5% |
| France | 60% | 60% | 74.5% |
| Germany | 38% | 38% | 50.5% |
| Greece | 53.7% | 53.7% | 53.7% |
| Indonesia | 34% | 62% | 65.5% |
| Switzerland | 24% | 42% | 42% |

Source: Figures from OECD (2017) "Pensions at a glance", pp.103 and 109.
*Figures adjusted in line with Danish Ministry of Finance (https://www.fm.dk/oekonomi-og-tal/oekonomisk-analyse/2017/det-danske-pensionssystem-nu-og-i-fremtiden), graphs 4.49 and 4.55. **An additional 4.5% income comes from ATP pension. Danish Ministry of Finance, ibid.

state pensions in the developed world (see table 1.1), and that the cushion of a historically large DB workplace system is fast deflating, and would assume that rules to make sure that our DC workplace pension system delivers a reliable income for middle and lower income pensioners in retirement are in place – but this is not the case.

## CONTRIBUTION LEVELS AND COVERAGE

An important factor in average pension outcomes relates to the level of contribution. UK automatic enrolment contributions from employer and employee are relatively low. The figures for the countries in this volume are: UK (8%), Canada (9.9%), Chile (10%), Denmark (12%), France (21.25%), Germany (18.9%), Greece (20%), Indonesia (8.7%, but possible future glidepath increases of 0.3% a year), and Switzerland (26.6%).

However, replacement rates will be a misleading indication of retirement outcomes if few people are actually participating.

Countries with large informal economies, like Indonesia in this volume, have low participation rates. More developed countries are struggling to incorporate the increasing number of self-employed workers into pension schemes, the UK included. Germany has had a relatively low participation rate in company schemes with only around half of the workforce in a workplace scheme. The new reform package in Germany is intended to address this.

Denmark, like Australia, provides an example of a country where contributions reached a higher level than in the UK via very small but regular incremental increases in annual contribution rates.

## GOVERNANCE

The chapter on the Swiss system emphasises how governance with strict rules to prevent conflicts of interest and fiduciary governance is considered vital to ensure both outcomes and the legitimacy of the workplace pension system. The Danish chapter also emphasises that similar factors are part of the success of the system, where workplace pensions have been developed in partnership between employers and trade unions over the last 28 years.

It is observable in the UK that differences in governance structures give rise to different levels of pricing. Data from the government's Department of Work and Pensions (DWP) shows that the mean cost of membership to a member in a master trust regardless of the size of the scheme is a 0.45% annual management charge (AMC). The mean cost of membership of a contract-based scheme depends on the size of the employer. This is striking given that the contract is nominally supposed to be with the individual. For employers with 1–5 employees, the mean AMC is 0.72%; 6–11 employees 0.69%; 12–99 employees 0.65%; 100–999 employees 0.56% and over 1,000 employees 0.45%[5]. (Note that half of all UK private sector employment is in firms that employ fewer than 50 people[6].)

## SCALE

The majority of employees in the UK are now served by DC pension schemes. There are approximately 14.1 million employees actively saving into DC workplace schemes, 8.5 million into trust-based schemes and 5.6 million into contract-based ones. A further 1.3 million are saving into hybrid DB and DC schemes and 680,000 into DB schemes[7].

The vast majority of low and medium earners automatically enrolled into a workplace pension scheme are in a DC scheme, and the vast majority of those members are with four providers: the National Employment Savings Trust (NEST), NOW-Cardano, the Legal and General Master Trust and The People's Pension. There is, however, also a long tail of small, often individual company schemes. The Pensions Regulator (TPR) estimate that there are just over 33,000 DC schemes in total in the UK, and about 2,010 schemes with more than 12 members, of which only 60 have more than 5,000[8].

There are scale benefits that accrue to pension schemes, which serve to lower costs and increase the returns to members' savings. These can potentially occur at two levels: at the administration layer, and, at the investment layer. Self-reporting by small schemes to TPR's annual surveys continues to demonstrate a struggle to provide adequate governance and to assess value for money[9].

The total costs at the administration layer do not rise much as additional members are added (e.g. the size and cost of operating the board of trustees and advisers to the board can potentially be fairly similar, regardless of the size of the scheme). As a consequence, the cost per member drops as each additional member joins. Indeed, there is no evidence of any real limit to the benefits of scale in this layer[10].

At the investment layer, scale enables pension schemes to negotiate more effectively with asset managers and to drive down the costs of the latter. In addition, scale that goes above a certain level allows pension schemes to take some investment services, such as infrastructure investment, in-house. The costs of doing so can be up to a third of what financial institutions would charge[11], and, diversification into this kind of less liquid asset may increase returns to members' savings.

In Canada, a 2012 report on scale in Pension Schemes for the Deputy Prime Minister and Minister of Finance found that schemes needed to have $CAD 50bn under management to operate most efficiently. The paper strongly endorsed the in-sourcing of functions to reduce costs, stating that:

> *"While a costly and complex undertaking, internal investment and risk management is widely seen as key to lowering costs and improving control and performance, provided it is appropriate based on investment objectives, has the ability to recruit and retain expertise at competitive rates, and has sufficient assets under management. Much of the recognized success of the large Canadian public-sector pension funds has come through the implementation of internal management."*[12]

In France and Greece, where the state is moving from a DB pay-as-you-go state-provided workplace pension to a notional-defined-contribution state-provided workplace pension, it is unclear how additional non-state workplace pensions will be able to generate the scale necessary to ensure low costs. Germany, like the Netherlands and Denmark, is likely to see the roll-out of industry and sector-wide pension schemes.

As the primary source of scale advantages are administration and investment management, scale is therefore potentially applicable to the retirement phase as well as the accumulation phase.

## COSTS AND CHARGES, DEGREE OF TRANSPARENCY

The UK has moved comparatively rapidly to require cost disclosure from trust-based DC schemes, both in terms of direct charges and indirect transaction costs incurred by underlying fund managers. The Local Government Pension Scheme has been active in setting out a template for disclosure. The requirement for full disclosure from those running trust-based DC schemes was adopted in April 2018[13]. Of the countries studied in this report, Denmark and Switzerland have also been leading protagonists. Unsurprisingly, this has in the past been less of a focus in countries such as France and Greece where the state has been the main workplace pension provider. This may be an area where the pioneering activity in Denmark, Switzerland, the Netherlands and now potentially the UK could provide case studies for other countries seeking to provide greater transparency.

## NOTES

1. The FCA research estimated that switching would rise from 8% of participants to 25% only. FCA (2016) "Implementing information prompts in the annuity market", p.26.

2. Weir, J. and Clacher, I. "The Default Option" in Bright Blue and the Fabian Society (2017) "Saving for the future", p.11.

3. FCA (2018) Retirement Outcomes Review. Final report, p.6.

4. OFT (2013) "Defined contribution workplace pension market study, p.167.

5. See table 3.3. in DWP (2017) Pension Charges Survey 2016: Charges in defined contribution pension schemes.

6. House of Commons Library, Briefing Paper Number 06152, 28 December 2017 Business statistics, p.5.

7. The Pensions Regulator, "DC Trust: presentation of scheme return data 2018–2019".

8. The Pensions Regulator, "DC Trust: presentation of scheme return data 2018–2019".

9. http://www.thepensionsregulator.gov.uk/press/smaller-dc-schemes-struggle-to-demonstrate-they-provide-value-for-pension-savers.aspx

10. Bikker, J. (2013) "Is there an optimal pension fund size? A scale-economy analysis of administrative and investment costs." DNB Working paper 376.

11. Bikker, J. A., O. W. Steenbeek, and F. Torracchi (2012). The impact of scale, complexity, and service quality on the administrative costs of

pension funds: A cross-country comparison. Journal of Risk and Insurance 79 (2), 477–514.

12. Ontario Ministry of Finance (2012) "Facilitating pooled Asset Management for Ontario's public-sector institutions." Paper from the Pension Investment Advisor to the Deputy Premier and the Minister of Finance.

13. The trustees of the People's Pension began publishing a full disclosure of all costs including transaction costs in September 2017: https://bandce.co.uk/technical-note-transaction-costs-disclosure/

# CANADA'S RETIREMENT INCOME SYSTEM

*Its strengths and weaknesses*

Keith Ambachtsheer

## LOOKING AT CANADA'S (R)ETIREMENT (I) NCOME (S)YSTEM FROM THE OUTSIDE IN

The Melbourne-Mercer Global Pension Index (MMGPI) assigns country ratings based on the assessed adequacy, sustainability, and integrity of its Retirement Income System (RIS) on a scale of 0–100. Canada's RIS achieved a 68 rating in 2018. The total 2018 rating range was 80–39 for 34 countries. Below the two 'A' ratings for the Netherlands and Denmark, Canada's 68 rating ranked tenth, one of 11 'B' ratings out of the total of 34. The common characteristic for the countries with higher ratings than Canada was compulsory participation in second pillar occupational pension plans.

How could Canada increase its RIS quality rating? The MMGPI creators have three recommendations:

1. Increase pension coverage through the development of attractive products for workers without occupational pension plans.
2. Increase savings rates for middle income earners.

3. Increase labour force participation rates at older ages as life expectancy increases.

And how do things look from the inside out?

## A LOOK AT CANADA'S RIS FROM THE INSIDE OUT

Canada's RIS structure roughly fits the World Bank's three-pillar model:

- Pillar 1: The Universal Old Age Security (OAS) program provides an inflation-indexed base pension to all Canadians aged 65 and over (currently about C$7,200 per year). This amount can vary based on income levels and marital status. Low-income Canadians may qualify for an additional Guaranteed Income Supplement (GIS) up to C$10,500, while at the high end of the income spectrum, the OAS pension is gradually clawed back starting at a C$76,000 income level and reaching 100% claw back at C$123,000.
- Pillar 2: Virtually all four million public sector workers are members of a DB-type plan, but out of 13 million private sector workers, only one million are members of a DB plan, and two million are members of a registered DC or hybrid DB/DC plan. Some 10 million workers are not members of a registered workplace pension plan at all (although they are members of the Canada Pension Plan, or of the Quebec Pension Plan if they are residents of Quebec. This is explained below).
- Pillar 3: The 10 million workers who are not members of a second pillar plan can save for retirement through tax-deferred Registered Retirement Savings Plans (RRSPs) or through Tax-Free Savings Accounts (TFSAs) where after-tax savings can be invested without incurring any further taxes upon withdrawal. RRSPs must be converted into Registered Retirement Income Funds (RRIFs) by age 71. Holders must withdraw at least a minimum amount from their RRIF as taxable pension income. About two-thirds of these

10 million workers have accumulated assets in one or more registered retirement savings vehicles.

However, this three-pillar description of Canada's RIS is incomplete. Through the creation of the Canada Pension Plan (CPP) and the Quebec Pension Plan (QPP) in the 1960s, the country created an additional pillar between pillars one and two. We might call it Pillar 1.5.

- Pillar 1.5: CPP/QPP are supplemental workplace-based pension arrangements requiring compulsory participation by employers and working Canadians. The original target income replacement rate was 25% of average earnings up to a maximum earnings level (currently about C$55,000). Originally a pay-go system, it was moved to a partially pre-funded basis in the 1990s, permitting a stabilized contribution rate of 9.9% of pay, split equally between employers and employees (the rate remains unchanged). In 2016, recognizing that the majority of private sector workers were not members of employer-sponsored pension plans, Canada's federal and provincial governments agreed to increase the target CPP/QPP benefit to 33% of average earnings, and increased the ceiling on maximum earnings covered by 14% (from C$55,000 to C$63,000). These enhancements are to be fully prefunded with the required additional contributions phased in over a number of years, starting in 2019. These enhancements will eventually raise the maximum CPP/QPP benefit from C$13,600 today to $20,400 in current dollars.

Just as the CPP/QPP are part of Canada's RIS is positioned between the first and second pillars, there is, arguably, another part positioned between pillars two and three:

- Pillar 2.5: This covers situations where employers play a role in creating a group RRSP arrangement for their workers. Here employers are involved in selecting a financial services organization to manage the group RRSP, and may also match employee contributions into their RRSPs up to some maximum amount. While it would seem logical for Canadian financial organizations to organize and sponsor these group RRSP arrangements themselves, they have been reluctant to do so for a combination of regulatory, risk-mitigation, and business model-related reasons.

Canada's RIS pays out some C\$220 billion annually in pensions: C\$50 billion through the first pillar OAS/GIS, \$60 billion through the Pillar 1.5 CPP/QPP, \$80 billion through second pillar workplace pension plans, and \$30 billion through pillar 2.5 and three Registered Retirement Income Funds RRIFs). Collectively, this represents about 11% of Canada's C\$2 trillion GDP. Looking ahead, the CPP/QPP and RRIF sectors are likely to see the most growth due the CPP/QPP benefit enhancements, the continued decline of DB plans, and the rapid transition of RRSP assets into RRIFs as Canada's population ages.

## IMPROVING CANADA'S RIS

Canada has already begun to act on MMGPI's three recommendations:

1.  CPP/QPP pensions will slowly increase over the coming decades, funded by rising CPP/QPP contribution rates starting in 2019, due to a Federal-Provincial agreement reached in 2016.
2.  Two existing occupational pension plans in the public sector have begun to offer their pension management infrastructure and balance sheets as a means for private sector employers to continue to offer their employees cost-effective collective pension plans without underwriting future balance sheet risks. Such an agreement has just been announced between the pension plan for college educators CAAT and the private sector media corporation Torstar. At the same time, a new pension delivery organization Common Wealth has begun to offer collective low-cost

multi-employer retirement savings programmes to employer/ employee groups in specific segments of Canada's labour market. For instance, its My65+ offering is for low income health care workers in Ontario, and its Common Good Plan is for Canada's entire not-for-profit employer/employee sector. Early responses to these two initiatives have been very positive.

3. Statistics Canada reports that while the proportion of the Canadian population over 65 has increased from 13% to 17% over the last 15 years, the proportion of senior Canadians reporting working income has also increased from 8% to 14%. However, Canada still lacks a clear retirement age policy, although there are incentives for delaying receipt of the OAS and CPP/QPP pension to age 71. At the same time, there is also still a lack of clear policy direction on post-retirement income support for low wage earners.

Two other positive developments worth noting are:

1. The evolution in collective public sector pension plans at the provincial and local levels from one-sided, fully-guaranteed DB plans to softer versions where risks are more evenly and fairly shared between tax/rate payers, employers, active workers, and retirees. The world leading Ontario Teachers Pension Plan, for example, has recently added conditional inflation protection (CIP) on future service to its arsenal of long-term plan sustainability levers. This CIP risk lever, which potentially reduces real benefits paid to retired as well as active teachers if the Plan is underfunded, falls directly on plan members. The main exceptions are the federal public service, military, and police (RCMP) plans. There is a perception in the country that the apparent inability of the federal government to reform their own second pillar pension arrangements may be due to Upton Sinclair's observation over 100 years ago that "it is difficult to get a man to understand something when his salary depends on not understanding it". Given the financial incentive not to understand, it

remains to be seen if this 'gold plated pensions' issue at the federal level will ever be resolved.

2. The continued evolution of the 'Canada model' of pension organization structure. The Model was first implemented in the early 1990s through the reorganization of the Ontario Teachers' Pension Plan. Other large Canadian pension organizations have since adopted the same model. Through reconfiguring mission, governance, and organizational structure, Canada Model pension organizations deliver measurably more 'value-for-money' in their investment management and benefit administration functions than alternative structures. A key element has been emphasizing scale and insourcing of the investment function, thus achieving superior performance at lower costs[1]. The model has become a standard that pension organizations in other countries aspire to. To date, it is only operating in federal/provincial-level government/public sector contexts.

Despite these positive developments, six challenges remain in Canada's RIS.

## SIX REMAINING CHALLENGES

Six remaining Canadian RIS challenges are:

1. Lack of integrated political decision-making and regulation. To cite just one example, there is no transparent, integrated protocol between the Federal/Provincial governments, the federal regulator's Office of the Chief Actuary, and the CPP Investment Board for working through and clearly communicating the CPP funding and investment policy implications of CPP benefit enhancements agreed on in 2016. There is also federal/provincial regulatory fragmentation between the pension and insurance sectors, and between individual and group investment regulations. Similarly, there is significant fragmentation at the academic, professional,

industry levels in both thought-leadership and action-leadership. One consequence is the slow, halting approach to innovation in Canada's RIS.

2. Continued lack of second pillar pension coverage. Out of a total of 17 million working Canadians, 10 million are still not members of a second pillar occupational pension plan, placing them at a considerable disadvantage to the 7 million who do have such a plan. Multiple research studies suggest their third pillar RRSP/TFSA/RRIF retirement savings pots will underperform those managed through second pillar collective pension plans by an average net return of 2%–3% per year. Over 40–60 year accumulation/decumulation periods, this results in a 40–50% reduction in ultimate pension payments. There is a misleading narrative that this underperformance is due to the superior DB relative to DC plan design. This is incorrect. Instead, it is due to conflicted and ineffective implementation infrastructure relative to more fiduciary and effective alternatives. Stated differently, using the 'Canada Model' for the implementation of any pension design will produce superior outcomes relative to biased, inefficient implementation models without a 'fiduciary duty' mindset, good governance, and scale[2].

3. Conflicts of interest and lack of expertise in third pillar pension provision. Regulatory efforts to protect individual Canadians saving for their own pillar three supplemental pension have been weak. Recent decisions by legislators and regulators to continue to permit 'financial advisors' to collect trailer and redemption fees on mutual fund sales is just the most recent example of this timidity. Further, a recent academic study found that in addition to having conflicts of interest, the average financial advisor also lacked the skill and temperament to deliver the services clients pay for[3].

4. Barriers to acquiring longevity insurance. There are also material legislative/regulatory barriers to individual Canadian retirement savers acquiring longevity risk insurance (i.e., against the risk of outliving their money) through a) being able to defer receiving

their OAS/CPP/QPP pensions above the current age-71 ceilings; b) through the provision of collective variable longevity risk-pooling arrangements; or c) through the provision of long-dated deferred annuity contracts by insurance companies. A broad coalition of RIS participants is currently addressing this short-coming, with a letter sent to the Finance Minister, Bill Morneau, outlining the problem and how it can be solved[4]. At the same time, further research and education efforts are required to help Canadians who are not members of DB plans understand the value of acquiring longevity insurance.

5. <u>Federal government second pillar pensions</u>. At the other end of the RIS spectrum, members of the federal public service, military, and RCMP pension plans continue to accumulate guaranteed final earnings-based, inflation-indexed pensions. The value of these pension promises continues to be materially understated in Canada's financial accounts. The Auditor General has pointed out that the balance sheets of these federal government second pillar pension plans continue to be subjected to material mismatch risk with, apparently, no-one accountable for establishing and managing an explicit risk policy for these plans. Meanwhile, these plans continue to receive preferential tax and regulatory treatments. As noted, this in turn leads to public sector workers receiving free guarantees underwritten by taxpayers, and material understate-ment of the cost of public sector pensions in the public accounts[5].

6. <u>Lack of clear policies on retirement age and support for low-income workers.</u> One of the policy planks of the opposition Liberal Party was to reverse the Conservative Government's decision to gradually raise the official retirement age from 65 to 67. That reversal occurred when the Liberals won the 2015 elec-tion. It remains to be seen where the retirement age issue goes in the coming years. Similarly, various proposals have been made to ensure that low-income workers are not disadvantaged by being encouraged or required to save for retirement only to see their income-tested Guaranteed Retirement Income Supplement reduced in retirement.

All this raises the question about how these remaining Canadian pension challenges are best addressed.

## ADDRESSING CANADA'S REMAINING PENSION CHALLENGES

There is today no single, integrated approach to identifying Canada's remaining pension challenges, proposing solutions to them, and then proactively devising strategies to see them through to implementation. Instead, there are occasional 'ad hoc' initiatives to identify issues and solutions, and to see those solutions through to implementation. While the current 'ad hoc' approach is far better than doing nothing, it does raise the question of a possible 'better way' for Canada.

Looking outside Canada, Australia and Finland offer two interesting 'better way' organizational structures, both of which I have worked with in the last few years:

1. Australia's *Productivity Commission* is an independent research and advisory arm of its federal government on a range of economic, social, and environmental issues affecting the welfare of Australians. It has placed the Australian RIS under a microscope over the course of the last two years and has just issued a report making a series of recommendations on how to improve the Australian RIS.

2. Finland's *Centre for Pensions* (Eläketurvakeskus) is a statutory co-operative created by Finland's national government. Its mandate to conduct research and provide advice to the government, the pension regulator, employers, and pension providers on how to enhance the sustainability, reliability, fairness, and efficiency of Finland's RIS. It issues regular reports on one or more of these topics.

These are two possible 'better way' models for Canada to consider in a longer-term timeframe.

Meanwhile, there is more immediate action underway to raise the level of innovation in Canada's RIS in the coming years:

1. Thought Leadership: Canada is not short on talented people thinking about and researching RIS questions. Through the National Institute on Aging (NIA), efforts are under way to create more frequent and effective opportunities for these people to interact with each other and reach consensus on how best to address Canada's remaining RIS challenges.

2. Action Leadership: good ideas that gain broad acceptance should be put into practice. This 'translation' process has not been working as well as it could in Canada. However, through the NIA, efforts are underway to create 'coalitions of the willing' on a 'good idea-by-good idea' basis. A recent example here is a 'longevity risk pooling coalition' involving six different organizations representing multiple constituencies: pensioners, pension organizations, insurance organizations, the actuarial profession, and academia. This is probably the broadest RIS coalition ever assembled in Canada. More will follow to address the six Canadian RIS challenges listed above.

Canada's retirement income system has many good features but also a number of well-identified challenges. Hopefully, these remaining challenges will be constructively addressed in the years ahead.

## NOTES

1. See my 2016 book *The Future of Pension Management* (Wiley) for more on the Canada Model.

2. 'Saving retail retirement investors. What will it take', in 'The Ambachtsheer Letter' (KPA, Oct 2018).

3. See the article 'Costly Financial Advice: Conflicts of Interest or Misguided Investment Beliefs?' by Linnainmaa, Melzer, Previtera (2015).

4. See http://www.cia-ica.ca/docs/default-source/2018/218120e.pdf for the contents of the Morneau letter.

5. See 'The Surprising Hidden Costs of Federal Employee Pensions', Robson and Laurin, and 'Ottawa Comes Part-Way Clean on its Pensions', Robson, C.D. Howe (2018), for a more detailed exposition of these issues.

# CHILE

## *The retirement income system*

## Jonathan Callund

### GENERAL DESCRIPTION

The Chilean pension system – widely known as the AFP (*Administradoras de Fondos de Pensions*)[1] system – came into being in 1981. As part of the last major reform in 2008, the multiple systems of state-funded minimum pensions were amalgamated into a 'solidarity' pillar and so, in broad terms, Chile now has a World Bank–style three-pillar pension system, with the second pillar deriving from mandatory contributions to pension savings accounts, and the third from tax-deferred voluntary individual (mostly) and employer savings[2].

The AFPs set up in law as private, for-profit organisations with a unique and strict objective to manage third-party pension savings in accounts – *Cuentas de Capitalizacion Individual*[3] – and related member services, subject to oversight of a technical *Superintendencia de Pensions*[4]. Each AFP manages a single and legally distinct portfolio – the *Fondo de Pensiones*[5], which is a unitized investment portfolio (akin to a unit trust/mutual fund) deriving from the contributions paid-in by its members and returns generated thereon. Since August 2002, however, each AFP has had to offer five sub-funds (*Multifondos*) with differing risk profiles and allow their members to select the fund where their pension savings are to be held, with the corresponding differentiated portfolio risks and returns. Switching between funds can be done at any time and as many times as a member chooses. There is no cost for switching fund and a member may also opt to split the fund into two subaccounts. In practice all AFPs offer their members on-line account management thus facilitating the switching process.

All employees must select and become a member of a single AFP, although members may then switch every six months. As of 2008, this process was simplified for first-time employees so that for the first 24 months of employment they are now automatically enrolled in the AFP that was selected as the cheapest in a bi-annual public tender process. Thereafter employees are free to switch to any AFP of their choosing.

From the outset, the AFP system led to some fundamental changes. First, the 32 industry- or employment-based *Cajas de Previsión*, which offered a multiplicity of defined benefit-type arrangements were wound up or closed to new members, and subsequently amalgamated into a single state entity – *Insituto de Normalizacion Previsional*. Prior to the reform, contributions – averaging from 35% to 45% of payroll – were shared between the employer and employees with the rates varying depending on the employee's *Caja*. After the reform, all wages were grossed up, transferring the onus of contributions for old age, disability, survivors' pensions, as well as healthcare, to salaries so that all contributions would be deducted from earnings. This had the underlying legal effect of ensuring employee property rights to their contributions, thus strengthening the enforcement and collection process.

Social security contributions are retained on a pay-as-you-earn basis at source by the employer, which is obligated to transfer the funds to an AFP. All contributions are deductions from gross monthly pay, subject to a ceiling currently Ch$2,225,582[6] (around US$3,070). The contribution rate for old-age retirement savings is 10%, which is credited to member's *Cuenta de Capitalizacion Individual*, and accumulates óver the members' working lives to become their primary source of retirement income. Normal retirement ages are 60 for women and 65 for men. However, retirement can take place beforehand once certain strict criteria are met.

Where a member is incapacitated or dies before they reach the age of retirement, the AFP system provides a two-stage process. First, the law provides for a special group insurance programme – *Seguro de Invalidez y Sobreviencia* (SIS) to meet the shortfall – *Aporte Adicional* – between the member's AFP account balance and the technical cost of providing a defined level of pension benefits based on the member's average earnings over the previous ten years. The *Aporte Adicional* is paid by the insurance companies into the member's AFP account and the member and/or survivors are then free to purchase an equivalent pension in the open annuity market.

The AFPs charge commission for managing members' accounts and these are an additional charge on the member's pre-tax earnings, currently ranging from 0.77% to 1.45% salary depending on the AFP. The cost of the SIS cover is paid by the employer and is currently a flat premium of 1.53% salary.

As such, there are three types of assured pension – old-age annuitants (for members retiring early or at normal retirement age), disability annuitants (for those members declared partially or totally disabled) and survivor annuitants (for spouses and children).

The state offers members two guarantees:

- In the case of old-age pensioners, and on condition that the member has at least 20 years' contributions, the state guarantees a *Pensión Básica Solidaria de Vejez*[7] (PBSV)[8]. In the case of disability or survivor pensioners, the conditions are reduced to 10 years' contributions, or two years' contributions in the five years prior to a claim, if and only if contributions were made in the month of the claim in the case of an accident. In any event, the survivors of retired members are entitled to the corresponding state PBSV.
- Where the member has acquired an annuity and the insurer is declared insolvent, the state guarantees the minimum pension, plus 75% of the contracted pension up to the social security ceiling.

At retirement, members have many options for drawing down their AFP funds. The decision is complex, given that the funds may only be taken in pension form based on joint member and dependents' life expectancies.

The first option is to leave the funds with an AFP and to draw down an actuarial annuity equivalent each month, the amount of which is reassessed each year. The second option is to transfer the balance to a life insurance company in return for a life-long guaranteed inflation-indexed annuity. To compound the complexity, there are then six AFPs and 15 annuity providers from which to choose.

Another big challenge is how to ensure that prospective pensioners have access to unbiased information and at minimal cost; to ensure they can make the best decision for themselves. Without a doubt, this is the most important financial decision a member will ever take. Given the mandatory nature of the system of individual pension savings, the onus is clearly on the state to ensure a level playing field.

Finally, the most important public policy challenge has been to ensure that the provider market is competitive and offers pensioners value when compared with other retirement options.

## MODES OF PENSIONS

All pensions in the AFP system are denominated in real terms in units (*Unidades de Fomento* (UF)). As such, the peso value is adjusted in line with domestic consumer price inflation and is determined as the number of UFs multiplied by the UF-value on the day of payment.

On meeting the conditions needed to retire, the first decision is whether to purchase an annuity (an annual retirement income featuring longevity insurance) or leave the balance with an AFP. In the case of the annuity – *Renta Vitalicia* – there are then multiple types: an immediate annuity versus a deferred annuity, and then with or without a guarantee. The law also recognises and dictates strict terms for three modes of annuity product.

*Renta Vitalicia Inmediata*: an immediate annuity with or without guarantees where the member instructs the AFP to transfer the account balance to a specialist life insurance company of their choice in return for a UF-denominated life annuity and contingent survivors' pensions for beneficiaries. This is an irrevocable decision.

*Renta Temporal con Renta Vitalicia Diferida:* a temporary income with deferred annuity, with or without guarantees, where the member leaves a portion of the balance with the AFP to fund pension income until the deferred annuity comes into effect. As such, this is a complex mathematical arrangement, complicated further by the legal requirement that, for the retirement pension, the UF value of the deferred annuity may not be less than 50% or greater than 100% of the value of the first temporary income drawdown from the AFP. In the case of survivor pensions under this mode, the first temporary income drawdown must be the same as the UF value of the deferred annuity.

*Renta Vitalicia Inmediata con Retiro Programado:* an income drawdown with immediate annuity, with or without guarantees, where the member splits the AFP balance between taking income drawdowns and an immediate annuity, receiving both payments simultaneously. The terms of the immediate annuity are as above. However, the balance held with the AFP remains the member's property and can subsequently then be transferred to another AFP or event to other financial intermediaries or can even be used to purchase a second annuity.

As to enhancements and guarantees, the AFP law allows members to add two types of endorsements to the basic policy terms. The most prevalent is a guarantee to continue payment of the original UF value of the member's pension for a given number of months after their death. Over 80% of annuities opt for guarantees ranging from five to 20 years, with the norm being a guarantee of 10 to 15 years[9]. The other is to agree a clause that enhances the value of a spouse's contingent pension, assessed in law[10] as 60% of the member's pension, to 100% of the pension.

The technical cost of each of these annuity products and the guarantee endorsements is markedly different. However, all of them will guarantee a life-long stream of inflation adjusted pensions for the member.

The option for an income drawdown – **Retiro Programado** – from an AFP, although also denominated in UF and based on joint life expectancies each year, offers no longevity cover and the value of a pension will tend to fall significantly in the medium term. In this sense, the drawdown option is primarily a temporary one as members will eventually see the value in opting for an annuity. As such, the majority of *Retiro Programado* is also a stock of future annuitants. There are two exceptions: the first group comprises members in poor health who prefer either to leave the decision on how best to draw their pensions to their dependents or, if there are no legal beneficiaries, leave the AFP balance as part of the deceased's estate, with a special tax allowance of UF4,000. The other large group, however, comprises members whose pension is less than the state minimum pension – *Pensión Básica Solidaria de Vejez* (PBSV). In these cases, currently accounting for two-thirds of retirees – the rule is that members are obliged to draw down a *Retiro Programado* equal to the PBSV until the AFP balance is exhausted. At this point, the state steps in and begins to pay said guaranteed pension.

## SCOMP AND THE RETIREMENT PROCESS

Given the complexity and public concern over the lack of transparency in the retirement process and in the role of intermediaries, the government introduced a radical change in 2002 with the creation of a new private entity to manage the process of tendering and member selection of pension products and providers (both AFPs and insurance companies). The AFP Association and the Insurance Association were invited to create a new legal entity – *Sistema de Consultas y Ofertas de Montos de Pension* (SCOMP) SA. This new agency is overseen by the Pension and Insurance Regulators and has managed all pensions transactions since January 2003.

Insurance companies are prohibited from offering annuities directly without going through this new exchange. Likewise, companies were banned from paying brokers' commissions of more than UF60 or 2% of premiums, whichever is less. Moreover, the legislation imposes strict prohibitions and penalties on the corporate officers, employees, agents, brokers or any other individuals involved in the sale of annuities to ensure that this limit is not breached.

Access to SCOMP and support in the process is provided exclusively through the member's AFP, thereby reducing the scope for the involvement of insurance agents or external pension advisers.

The AFPs and annuity providers are obliged to participate in this interconnected, electronic information-sharing system and publish their bids, thus allowing the member to receive consistent and comparable quotes on the conversion factors for their accrued pension savings.

The retirement process works as follows:

1. On reaching normal retirement age, or on meeting early retirement conditions, the member approaches his/her AFP and completes and signs a form requesting his or her pension together with a further form, confirming the existence of beneficiaries and so initiating the process of retirement. This process can be done alone (directly) or by being 'sponsored' by an insurance agent or external pension adviser, all of which have unique identity codes. If a third party is involved, then the agent or advisor is recorded as the *sponsor* in the process.

2. The AFP has 10 working days to compile the details and issue a certificate recording the member's name, sex, date of birth, ID number and address; the age, sex and type of dependants; the accumulated balance in the individual capitalisation account; and the nominal value and issue date of the *Bono de Reconocimiento*[11] (recognition bond). The certificate is valid for 35 days.

3. Before issuing the certificate, the AFP needs to:
   a. Review the member's contribution record and check with other AFPs that they are not holding any member contributions, for instance through employer error, and
   b. Assesses the member's entitlement to the annuity option, i.e. ensure the projected pension is equal to or greater than the

state minimum pension – *Pensión Básica Solidaria de Vejez* (PBSV). Those that do not meet this requirement are informed that their only option is a Programmed Withdrawal.

4.  The AFP sends a certificate to members with the annuity option – a physical copy is sent by certified mail to the member's home address on file and simultaneously SCOMP received an electronic copy – containing the details outlined in step 2, above. In the interim, SCOMP sets up the member's account on the system in anticipation of the requests for quotes.

5.  On receipt of the physical copy, the member then has can make three successive requests for quotations (i.e. the cycle of the first must be completed before a $2^{nd}$ and $3^{rd}$ can be initiated) by defining a mix of annuity options – there are over 25 permutations.[12]

    The *sponsor* is normally closely involved at this stage. The process is carried out online and the selections are submitted directly onto the SCOMP system, either by the AFP, the insurance agent or an external pension advisor, using their identity code. Commissions can be avoided if a member carries out the process directly in the office of an AFP or Insurance Company, without the support of an agent or pension advisor.

6.  On receipt of an online member request, SCOMP then sends out electronically a simultaneous request to all the insurance companies and AFPs – all of which have permanent Internet connections. They then have 8 days to submit their offers online.

7.  On closing the individual tender process, SCOMP then has four working days to send a *Certificado de Ofertas* by certified mail to the member's home address, detailing the range of offers received from the participating insurance companies and AFPs, together with instructions on how to proceed in each case, whether annuity or drawdown. Given their interest rate sensitivity, all annuity offers are valid for 12 working days from the closing date of the SCOMP process.

8.  With this, the members may:
    a.  Accept one of the **SCOMP offers**, and this need <u>not</u> be the cheapest;

b. Seek an *external* **offer** from one or more of the companies that (necessarily) participated in the SCOMP tender process – this new offer must be better than the original offer for the same policy terms from the same company and will also be registered on the SCOMP system;

c. Request a **re-run**, based on new product combinations (deferred period and/or guarantees) – the $2^{nd}$ or $3^{rd}$ request;

d. Initiate a **private tender** process, asking for quotes from at least three companies after having set a minimum price, which may in turn not be less than the best SCOMP quote. In this case, the member is obliged to accept the best offer, when at least two companies bid for the contract; or

e. Simply postpone any decision until a later date.

Offers arising under SCOMP, or where there is only one offer under the private tender, are not binding on the member, who may postpone any decision indefinitely.

9. A member has 15 days to accept an external offer from an insurance company. In the case of a private tender, the offer is valid for 10 days.

All offers are denominated in UFs and provide the unit pension cost, net of any brokerage commission. This unit pension cost is effectively the amount of capital required to purchase a pension of UF1 per month for the member's lifetime, including the cost of any contingent pensions for dependent survivors.

Where a member opts for a *Retiro Programado*, the AFP is obliged to provide information on the projected value of future monthly pensions (in UFs) for each of the years over the member's expected lifetime, based on the prevailing mortality tables and interest rates.

The closing process is no simpler either:

10. Until the process is closed, an agent or pension advisor may adjust/cede part of the sales commission/fee to enhance the member's pension. This process is transparent and reported to the AFP.

If sponsored by an agent, a member may always opt to go with an offer from another company and so avoid paying the sponsoring agent's commission. However, in the case of external offers, the member may opt for another company, and, in this case, the agent/advisor's commission/fee will be due.

11. The member is required to go to the AFP to select the pension method, and sign and accept the offer from the AFP or company. With this, the AFP then informs SCOMP, which in turn proceeds to inform the winner.

12. In the case of an annuity, the company then has three days to issue the electronic policy and send it to the member's AFP.

   Other than the details of any guarantees and/or deferred period, the policy conditions are standard and common to all companies, based on the pension law and regulations.

13. On receipt of the policy, the AFP then has 10 working days to transfer the funds to the company (*Renta Vitalicia*) or AFP (*Retiro Programado*).

## THE MARKET

The pension provider market comprises seven AFPs and 15 annuity companies.

AFPs currently (November 2018) have 10,9 million members (*Afiliados*) with individual AFP accounts, out of which 5,6 million active members (*Cotizantes*) make regular contributions, only 2% of which are self-employed.

As at August 2019[13], there were 1,394,427 members in receipt of pensions, of which:

- 719,104 were making AFP drawdowns;
- 45,693 were making temporary drawdowns, i.e. pending the start of a deferred annuity; and
- 617,833 were receiving life annuity payments.

In terms of the stock of pensioners by type of pension:

- 227,023 are in receipt of early retirement pensions;
- 739,098 receive normal retirement pensions;
- 284,790 receive survivors (widows and orphans) pensions; and
- 143,516 receive disability (total or partial) pensions.

On retirement, AFPs continue to manage their members' funds and pay the regular drawdowns – *Retros Programados* and *Rentas Temporales* – and charge commissions ranging from 0% to 1.25% of the monthly payment[14].

Insurance companies, however, factor their administration and risk charges into the unit price of the annuities they sell, less any commission/fee payable to the agent or pensions advisor.

The latest Pension Regulator report for the period January 2018 to December 2018[15] shows that of the 154,599 AFP members applying for retirement in those 12 months, only 51,461 (33%) were able to make use of the SCOMP exchange, given that the resulting pension entitlements of the majority was less than the state minimum pension. Of the SCOMP pensioners, 6% were due to early retirements; 74% for normal old-age retirement; 12% for disability; and 8% for survivors.

The majority (42%) of these pensions were drawn as temporary income with deferred annuity and the balance being split between AFP drawdowns (i.e. an indefinite deferment of the date to opt for an annuity) and an immediate annuity. Less than 0.2% of pensioners opted for an income drawdown with immediate annuity.

The average monthly pensions drawn following the SCOMP process for AFP drawdowns (in the first year), were UF15.2 (around US$590) for old-age, UF17.4 (US$674) disability and UF5.2 (US$200) for survivors. These compare with UF13.03, UF14.6 and UF5.7 respectively for immediate annuity pensions. That said, these average amounts disguise considerable variations depending on the individual's contribution history and earnings, which makes any relative comparisons difficult across groups and in relation to final earnings.

## ANNUITY DISTRIBUTION AND SEGMENTATION

As indicated, there are two primary distribution channels – agents and pension advisors.

Insurance company agents are tied or independent sales agents working directly with one of more annuity providers and are the primary sales channel, representing around half of all annuity sales over the last 15 years.

The pension advisers evolved out of specialist brokers, ex annuity agents, ex AFP employees and social workers who, after the reform of 2002, opted to take a technical exam to be certified by the Insurance Superintendent. They provide advice to AFP members, some throughout a member's working life although most often only immediately before a member comes to retire. At present there are 613 registered.

These intermediary channels are the prime source of advice to members leading up to and at retirement, offering valued services in educating members on their options and advising them through what is a complex process. The prime difference is that *a pension adviser* is not tied to a given company and has a mandate to impart impartial advice, and is not selling the product of any particular provider.

The latest Pension Regulator report shows that 44% of retirees opt not to use any intermediary in the retirement process. Insurance agents advised in 33% of cases and only 23% of retirees opted to be counselled by *pension advisers*. Once again, these rates disguise differences across the type of pension method – whereas only 4% of AFP drawdowns are set up with intermediary support, nearly 80% of annuities are placed with the help of an agent or pension adviser.

## COMPETITIVENESS OF CHILEAN ANNUITY MARKET

Assuming a relatively complete pensions contribution record throughout a member's working life, Chile's AFP system has been shown to provide retirees with some of the most competitive terms found anywhere. Annuity markets around the world have been assessed using the widely-recognised *Money's Worth Ratio (MWR)* methodology since the late 1990s and Chile has consistently been a leader, not least in the inflation-adjusted annuity segment.

MWR is a proxy for the relative value of long-term financial arrangements. It amounts to expected present discount rate (EPDR) of cash flows from an annuity divided by the initial premium when compared to the risk-free rate of financial instruments in a given market. A ratio of around 100% implies that an annuitant is getting good value.

Over the last 30 years there have been a range of international studies comparing annuity provision in markets such as the US, the UK, Germany, Switzerland, Canada, Singapore and Chile. Chile has usually come out on top of these international rankings. The most recent academic study was carried out in 2007[16]. In 2017 the Chilean *Fiscalía Nacional Económia* used the MWR as the basis for its detailed assessment of the Chilean annuity market and estimated MWR 'new' ratios for the period 2008–17[17], all of which indicate ratios of 105% to 108% of the risk-free rate.

## NOTES

1. Pension Fund Administrations.
2. The new first pillar was discussed in volume II of this series.
3. Individual capitalization accounts.
4. Pension regulator.
5. Pension fund.
6. Equivalent to UF79.3, where the UF – *Unidad de Fomento* – is consumer price inflation-linked unit of account quoted each day and used for most financial transactions. As at 24 October 2019, UF1 was equal to Ch$28,065.35 = £30.14 = €34.88 = US$38.73, where: £1 = Ch$931.02; €1 = Ch$804.56; US$1 = ChS724.70.
7. Basic old age solidarity pensions.
8. As at 1 July 2018 – the last date of adjustment – the PBSV was Ch$110.201 per month and is adjusted for once a year for consumer price

inflation in the previous 12 months, or immediately if inflation were to exceed 10% in a given period.

9. Table 11, p 74, FNE – Estudio de Mercado sobre Rentas Vitalicias (EM01-2017) – Santiago – Informe Final, February 2018.

10. Article 58 of D.L. N°3.500.

11. This is a state bond issued to *AFP* members who switched out of the 'old' pay-as-you-go pension system. The bond's nominal value is determined in relation to contributions made to the old system and accrues interest at a real rate of 4% p.a. from the date of switching.

12. Selection of the pension modes (outline in II above), for example, if deferred, for how many months and what proportion of the initial pension; if guaranteed, for how many months; and then there's an option to nominate special beneficiaries on death.

13. For further details on the system as at August 2019, see Ficha Estadistica Previsional N°83 – octubre 2019 – https://www.spensiones.cl/portal/institucional/594/articles-13763_recurso_1.pdf

14. For the fourth trimester of 2019, the AFP commissions, as a percentage of the monthly drawdowns, were set at: 1.25% for AFP Capital, AFP Cuprum and AFP Provida, 1.20% for AFP Uno and AFP Modelo, 0.95% for AFP Habitat and 0.00% for AFP Planvital – https://www.spensiones.cl/apps/estcom/estcom.php

15. Informe Semestral de Selección de Modalidad de Pensión; Superintendencia de Pensiones, September 18.

16. Thorburn, Craig, et al. (2007) "An Analysis of Money's Worth Ratios in Chile", Cambridge, Journal of Pension Economics and Finance 6 (3): 287–312.

17. Page 93, FNE – Estudio de Mercado sobre Rentas Vitalicias (EM01-2017) – Santiago – Informe Final – febrero de 2018.

# THE DANISH RETIREMENT INCOME SYSTEM

## Torben Möger Pedersen

The Danish pension system attracted international attention when it was ranked best in the world for the sixth straight year in 2017 by the annual Melbourne Mercer Global Pension Index (MMGPI) report, prepared and published by Mercer and the Australian Centre for Financial Studies. It took first place again in 2019.

Denmark's prominent ranking is the result of a first-class and robust pension system that provides good replacement rates, is sustainable and has a high level of integrity.

## THE PENSION SYSTEM IN GENERAL

The Danish pension system comprises three pillars: a basic state pension scheme plus means-tested supplementary pension, fully funded employer-paid pension schemes and voluntary private savings schemes.

The year 2018 marked the 25th anniversary of the introduction of labour-market (second pillar) pension schemes for large groups of skilled and unskilled workers in Denmark. Implementation was based on a tripartite agreement between the trade unions and

42

TORBEN MÖGER PEDERSEN

employers' associations (hereafter: called 'social partners') and the government that aimed to secure workers a supplement to the state pension in line with the pension schemes of most public-sector employees and a large number of private-sector white-collar employees and academics.

Less than half the labour force was estimated to have a pension scheme prior to 1990. However, pension scheme agreements covering a number of additional occupational groups that were made in the early 1990s mean that more than 90 per cent of the labour force (self-employed persons excluded) now have a pension scheme. This supplements their state pension and their pension from the mandatory ATP (Arbejdsmarkedets Tillægspension) pension scheme, (a scheme similar to the Canada Pension Plan in being a government managed scheme sitting between the first and second pillars, see the chapter on Canada in this volume).

The establishment of the new pension schemes was based on a tripartite agreement between the government and the social partners. The government's focus was mostly on improving the Danish economic situation, which was plagued by a lack of competitiveness and large and persistent current account deficits. The advantage of having the new arrangement agreed upon through collective bargaining rather than being implemented by legislation was that the new pensions contributions could – if the social partners agreed – be paid for by the foregoing of pay rises, thus avoiding increasing employers' total payroll costs by as much as would otherwise have been the case[1]. Over the years from 1993 to 2008 approximately one third of total payroll increases were in the form of pensions contributions.

In return for the social partners' commitment, the government promised to implement legislation to improve pension schemes for the unemployed and the sick. However, schemes for these groups have only just now been established with effect from 2020, though their ATP contributions have been increased.

Thus, with effect from 1993, pension schemes were established for large groups of skilled and unskilled workers – both in the private sector and public sector. To begin with, it was typically agreed that 0.9% of salary would be paid into a funded savings scheme, comprising both a life-long annuity and some minor insurance coverage. The social partners successfully prioritised using a substantial portion of pay increases over the subsequent 15 years to increase pension contributions, meaning that minor improvements typically were implemented each year so that contributions averaged 12% around ten years ago.[2] No significant adjustments have been made since then. Hence, another 40 years will be required before the schemes are fully mature and pension pay-outs reflect a full working life of saving.

It is therefore important to mention that the Danish state pension protects all citizens without savings against poverty. The state pension is divided into an income-dependent (means-tested) portion of DKK80,736 (US$12,390) per year (for single people and half that amount per head for cohabiting people) plus another DKK74,844 per year, which is not dependent on the person's income from private pension schemes. Thus, all citizens are secured a reasonable income as retirees, whether they have saved for their retirement or not. But means testing implies that citizens with their own savings do not benefit to quite the same extent from a state pension[3].

Overall, state pensions are still the principal income of Danish retirees. However, total payments from private pension schemes are expected to exceed state pensions within the coming 25 years, reflecting the extraordinary growth of the former.

## PLAYERS IN THE DANISH PENSION MARKET

Players in the Danish private pension market have a variety of corporate profiles. Firstly, there are a number of commercial companies that are typically part of a major financial group with a bank or a general insurance company parent. These companies account for approximately 40% of total annual contributions in pillars 2 and 3[4]. Secondly, there are commercial companies operating on a non-profit basis in the sense that their owners either do not get a share of the company's profit or the companies are owned by the customers. Nonetheless, they compete for both company pension schemes and private pension savings. These companies account for almost 25% of contributions.

The remaining roughly 35% of the market comprises member-owned "pension funds" and limited companies operating according to the same principles as the pension funds in that the boards of directors are composed of representatives of the members and contributing companies, while the customer group is well-defined and limited to one (or a few) specific occupational groups or sectors covered by collective agreements. These companies do not engage in direct sales efforts outside the covered occupational groups and are referred to as "labour market related pensions funds" with a special status in the financial regulations which means, among other things, that they are exempt from corporate tax.

Since 1981, pension funds have been subject to the same regulations as limited insurance companies despite, for instance, the main principles of the EU regulation distinguishing between a commercial business governed by the Solvency II rules and pension funds or *pensionskasser* which – generally – fall within the IORP (pension funds supervisor) directives. In Denmark, pension funds are subject to the Solvency II rules as well as legislation on financial enterprises, in the same way as commercial companies. This is based on the idea that the same product requires the same protection. And in practice, there is no difference between the products that may be provided by pension funds and life insurance companies.

In Denmark, there are only a very small number of company pension funds, which fall within the IORP rules for pension funds. Company pension funds administer pension schemes for employees of a single company or group and are often established as defined-benefit pension schemes, in contrast to the multi-employer occupational pension funds and all other private pension schemes in Denmark. Existing company pension funds are typically relatively small and closed to new members.

Even for company pension funds, the requirements of full funding and separation of pension fund assets from the assets of the sponsor company have, however, been a fundamental principle since 1935 when the first legislation on company pension funds was adopted.

## TAXATION OF PENSION SCHEMES IN DENMARK

Danish tax rules have also had a major impact on how pension schemes are set up. The underlying principle with respect to pensions is that contributions are tax deductible whereas payments are subject to income tax and offset against state benefits. ETT (exempt/taxed/taxed) is the main principle employed, but recent legislative amendments in this area will gradually lead to a mixed ETT/TTE system.

The rules governing the taxation of pensions are complicated and often amended. The current fundamental principle is, however, that contributions to lifelong annuities may be deducted from taxable income without limits. As regards schemes with other types of benefit pay-outs, contributions to pensions in periodic instalments of up to DKK54,700 (2018) are tax deductible, whereas schemes disbursed as a lump sum are not deductible.

Overall, the opportunities to save towards a lump sum payment are, in fact, rather limited. Reforms in recent years have both removed the possibility of deducting contributions to lump sum pension plans and, with effect from 2018, restricted the actual amount that may be paid into such plans. People who are more than five years away from entitlement to a state pension (in 2018 this means people under 60 years old) may only pay DKK5,100 annually into lump sum pension plans. People older than 60 may pay DKK46,000 into such plans in 2018, though the amount will increase to DKK51,100 over a five-year period.

The rules on taxation of pension disbursements cannot be evaluated without including the rules governing the income-dependent element of the state pension, as this also reduces the value of pension savings. Under Danish rules, both lifelong annuities and pensions in periodic instalments reduce the state pension if the annual disbursements exceed just over DKK20,000. In practice, this means that all disbursements up to DKK332,500 (for single people) from private pension schemes will reduce the state pension, as the ATP scheme is also included in the calculation and disbursements from ATP typically correspond to the basic allowance of just over DKK20,000. In contrast, lump sum payments do not lead to a loss of state pension entitlements. The amendments to the rules on lump sum payments have, together with an adjustment to the income tax system which increased the deductible value of payments into life-long annuities and pensions in periodic instalments, primarily had the purpose of ensuring that all workers can build up entitlement to regular retirement income streams that are efficient in the sense that they generate a higher total value compared with normal, non-pension savings and which do not significantly reduce state pension benefits.

Pension taxation rules also define the possibilities for converting savings after making payment, e.g. in connection with the transition to disbursement or at some other time. The overall principle is that such changes may only be made if the disbursement period is extended. More specifically, lump-sum savings may be converted to pensions in periodic instalments or lifelong annuities, and pensions in periodic instalments may be converted to lifelong annuities, but not vice-versa.

## DANISH RETIREMENT PENSION PRODUCTS

The emphasis on stable retirement income streams in the Danish system is therefore built on the following pillars. First, the tax rules agreed by parliament provide incentives for saving towards some form of regular, long-term (mainly lifetime) pension. Second, the rules governing the supervision of pension funds have historically accommodated the need for lifetime benefits through the requirement that at least 90 per cent of an individual's total contributions to the pension scheme should be used for lifelong annuities. Third, collectively bargained schemes have lifetime coverage at their core, as do public-sector first pillar collective agreements, where the employers (state, regions and municipalities) demand that the major part of contributions must be used for lifetime benefits. Fourth, the new defined-contribution schemes built in the 1990s, focused mainly on lifelong annuities.[5] With longer life expectancy and the resulting attention to the significance of lifelong benefits, demand for lifetime annuities is likely only to increase.

There is one aspect of the design of pension retirement products in Denmark which is distinctive and the subject of debate and indeed criticism from some quarters, and that relates to their not disbursing all savings to beneficiaries on the death of the insured. Longevity insurance in occupational pensions typically comprises an element of coverage at death (which disburses parts of savings to beneficiaries), but parts of remaining savings go back into the pool covering that specific generations pensions entitlements.

Retirement savings plans are also supplemented with various insurance coverages often built on principles of solidarity that does not differentiate on the basis of health, gender or, in some cases, even age. Since contributions only amounted to 0.9% of a worker's pay to begin with, the sums paid in were very small, and risk coverage was also naturally very modest. As contributions increased, insurance coverage was also improved. As standard, a modern Danish labour market pension scheme includes a right to regular disbursements as well as a premium waiver for policyholders who are granted a state anticipatory (disability) pension, and also a right to a lump sum of a defined amount on the death of the insured, the granting of an anticipatory pension, or in the case of critical illnesses. However, savings for a retirement pension, and particularly a lifetime retirement pension, are the most important element of the pension scheme, and the benchmark is that insurance coverage should account for a maximum of 20% of contributions.

## FROM GUARANTEED BENEFITS TO UNIT-LINKED SCHEMES

Originally, pension schemes typically offered guaranteed benefits, which in practice meant people were guaranteed relatively low benefits that would be stepped up if the pension fund achieved higher returns than predicted when the guaranteed benefits were calculated.

However, falling interest rates during the 2000s posed a challenge to guaranteed benefits. Danish companies had to make substantial provisions to meet their obligations as a result of declining market rates. At the same time, guaranteed benefits forced companies to pursue a prudent investment strategy, thus limiting the possibility of generating reasonable risk-weighted returns through investments in riskier assets. As a result, a majority of pension schemes have been converted to unit-linked principles over the past fifteen years.

Another advantage is that the solvency capital requirements under the risk-based Solvency II rules are less strict for unit-linked schemes than for guaranteed schemes. [6]

The principles underpinning this conversion vary from one company to the other and from one scheme to the other, as the conversion depends on the nature of the pension schemes. Schemes provided under collective agreements can often be converted with effect for all policyholders and the entire savings, both future and past contributions, by decision of the board of directors. This is possible if the board of directors is composed of representatives of all relevant parties of the underlying collective agreements (and if the board members are authorised to represent the relevant parties). In other cases, changes may be affected by a specific agreement between the parties to the collective agreement. This is based on the collective bargaining system, which, from a legal perspective, implies that the representatives of workers and employers are authorised to act on behalf of the individual worker or employer in the areas governed by the collective agreement.

The fact that the board of directors is composed of representatives of workers and employers also means it is competent to assess the composition of the pension scheme based on customers' needs. Moreover, the legal requirements regarding to the financial skills of boards have increased in recent years.

Other companies may have to obtain positive acceptance from individual policyholders to make such changes to an existing scheme. However, many people have accepted the change to a unit-linked scheme because the return potential will often be higher and because Danish law allows policyholders to transfer their share of the often considerable reserves to their own account in the unit-linked environment.

Fifteen years ago, less than 10% of total contributions went to unit-linked schemes. Today the ratio is around two-thirds. The transition to unit-linked schemes has meant that there is no longer a guaranteed minimum benefit from the scheme. This also means that the pay-out is adjusted (typically on an annual basis) depending on the investment return during the decumulation phase. The same goes for the expected payment during the accumulation phase.

Fortunately, favourable market trends over the past ten years following the financial crisis mean the unit-linked schemes have produced solid returns. Experience suggests policyholders acknowledge that the value of their savings may decline during periods of poor returns from the financial markets. Furthermore, monthly payments under schemes that were established 25 years ago (and which only matures 30-40 years from now) often amount to less than half of the state pension, so a decline in pension benefits would have a relatively small impact on the policyholder's total income. However, it remains to be seen how policyholders will react if the returns produced for their accounts turn out to be negative for a shorter or longer period. Naturally, declining benefits are more serious for policyholders who have already retired.

Creating stability in pension benefits by smoothing payments in various ways has been recognised as necessary. The goal is generally to provide stable benefit payments and under normal circumstances to track inflation, so pay-outs are only reduced from one year to the next if returns are very poor. This is typically achieved by retaining part of the individuals' savings as a buffer that will be used in case of poor investment returns and otherwise released over time. This buffer is unique to each individual not collective.

## CUSTOMERS' POSSIBILITIES FOR ADJUSTING THEIR PENSION SCHEMES

As mentioned, the Danish rules set out limited possibilities for changing the disbursement profile of a retirement savings plan. Moreover, it is quite common that individual policyholders can decide the scope of the insurance coverage and thus the allocation of total contributions between savings and insurance.

Another question raised in the political debate on pensions is whether policyholders should be able to influence how their own savings are invested in the unit-linked environment – a possibility many companies now offer. In practice, however, most policyholders prefer to let the company or the board of directors determine both the insurance coverage and the mix of investments. Consequently, ensuring that the default composition of the pension scheme is appropriate for a majority of policyholders is vital. Pension schemes forming part of a collective agreement may be designed so they match the (well-known) pay and working conditions of the customers. This allows for the establishment of good uniform insurance coverage with benefits on death, the granting of anticipatory pension or in the case of critical illnesses. This is well suited for the majority of the customers and reduces the consequences of their lack of motivation to make these decisions themselves.

Of course, efforts are made to improve the level of information and engagement among customers. All companies offer direct access to detailed information through personalized websites, often with a range of options to modify the content of the scheme digitally. Further advice is offered either through personal meetings or through information meetings in the workplace etc.

At retirement, the customer will most often choose to seek advice from the provider either through the website or by phone. Frequently the company will offer themed sessions targeted towards customers close to retirement.

This means customers will typically be advised by their own company or in some cases by their bank. A national service offering personal advice related to the choices embedded in the pension schemes has not been necessary.

However, the industry has developed a tool aimed at giving individuals an overview of their total savings and insurance coverage. This is done through a website[7] to which all Danish companies (and banks) report information on each customers' savings, projected benefits and insurance cover (on death, disability and critical illness). This gives individuals an opportunity to receive an overview of all pension plans, no matter which company they have been placed in. This is of particular value for individuals with frequent job changes

There is seldom a charge attached to any of these services from the pension provider as the costs are financed by the general administrative fees.

Extensive use of big data is another way to secure the best interests of members without relying on the individual member's own initiative. Digital solutions can be used to reach citizens who have been exposed to an event, which may, with a certain probability, entitle them to benefits from a pension scheme. This applies to pay-outs relating to anticipatory pension, death, critical illness or long-term illness. By coordinating public registers with data on the granting of anticipatory pension, death, diagnosis of serious illnesses or receipt of unemployment benefit due to long-term illness with data about the individual's insurance coverage, public authorities can contact the relevant citizen with information about their probable right to benefits from the pension scheme.

## TRANSPARENCY AND COST EFFICIENCY

The openness of pension and insurance companies has been a subject of debate for some years in Denmark, and there has been a wish from many quarters for greater transparency with respect to costs and returns. Many initiatives have been implemented that require companies to publish information on these matters that is suitable for comparison. Denmark is considered to have advanced considerably in this field compared with other countries.

Despite these many initiatives and the fact that a very large proportion of pension schemes are made under collective agreements where individual policyholders or businesses are unable to choose where the scheme should be placed, the market is seen to be efficient and cost levels are low. Pension schemes under collective agreements typically cost less than DKK500 (£60) per year for administration (excluding investment costs). The level is somewhat higher for older pension funds, around DKK700–800 (£95), whereas commercial companies typically charge around DKK2,000 (£235). The main reason for this difference is that commercial companies have a far more diverse range of products and offer one-on-one advisory sessions to individual customers in connection with the setting-up of the pension scheme.

## NOTES

1. A similar set of economic and social circumstances precipitated the creation of the Australian superannuation system in the early 1990s, discussed in volume 1 of this series, whereby pay rises were diverted into pension contributions.

2. The contributions are typically split with two-thirds paid by the employer and one-third by the employee.

3. The interaction between the Danish pensions pillars was discusses in detail in volume 2 of the current series.

4. The contributions in the third pillar is app. 10 pct. of the contributions in the second pillar.

5. However the small number of schemes established at company level tend to be based on lump-sum payments or pension in instalments rather than lifelong benefits.

6. Germany's recent enabling of unit linked DC arrangements reflects a similar set of circumstances. Discussed in detail in this volume.

7. pensionsinfo.dk

# THE FRENCH PENSION SYSTEM

## Christophe Albert and Anne Lavigne

The French pension system is often depicted as complex and fragmented but participation is actually quite straightforward for all citizens. The system is basically composed of two major pay-as-you-go
schemes, the general first pillar basic scheme – *Régime général* or
CNAV (Caisse Nationale d'Assurance Viellesse) – for most wage-
earners working in the private sector (representing 60–70% of the
labour force), and the public pension scheme that applies to civil servants and military personnel (representing about 15% of the labour
force). The apparent complexity arises from the existence of similar
sector specific schemes for particular groups of workers including
agricultural and self-employed workers, and special schemes for
workers in state-owned companies. For private-sector employees,
the first-pillar pay-as-you-go scheme is complemented by a workplace pay-as-you-go point-based scheme. In the worldwide landscape of pension systems, France is thus characterised by its high
level of coverage provided by the state-managed pension system and
its very low level of pension funding, either at the individual level
or at the workplace level. Current reforms are likely to change the
defined-benefit nature of the system, but the overall pay-as-you-go
dimension of the system will remain, with little room for private

sector defined contribution pension schemes at the workplace or personal level.

## THE HIGH LEVEL OF STATE PENSION COVERAGE

The first-pillar basic scheme provides a guaranteed annual income in retirement to all private sector wage-earners[1]. At retirement, a retiree receives a pension proportionate to the years of contribution and to a reference wage. The full-rate basic pension entitles claimants to up to 50% of their reference wage; it can be obtained either at age 62 with a contributory record of 41.5 years for the generation born in or before 1955 – although the contribution record will progressively increase up to 43 years for the generations born after 1972 – or at the age of 67 regardless of the contributory record.

Two complementary pay-as-you-go schemes provide additional pensions for private sector employees that top up their basic pension. ARRCO[2] (for all workers) and AGIRC[3] (for executive workers) schemes are mandatory and managed by the social partners (i.e. the trade unions and employer representatives). Contributions to these schemes enable workers to buy points throughout their career. The purchase price of a point is set by the scheme and determines how many points can be bought in exchange for yearly contributions; the service value of the point determines the level of pension derived from the amount of points accumulated by the time at which retirement takes place.

An equivalent two-pillar structure – *sécurité sociale des indépendants*[4] – exists for self-employed workers, with the same rules applying to the first-pillar pension as in the *régime général* and complementary points-based pensions provided by a wide array of dedicated professional schemes.

The public sector pension scheme is integrated, meaning it provides both a basic and a complementary (occupational) pension. It covers military personnel and civil servants in central, local and hospital administration and provides guaranteed annual incomes.

Some civil servants receive, in addition to their index-related salary, an additional pension outside the integrated pay-as-you-go scheme, in a mandatory fully-funded pension fund (*Retraite additionnelle de la fonction publique* or RAFP[5]). A civil servants' pension at full rate equals 75% of the last six months' salary, but the RAFP scheme only represents a very small percentage of their pension income.

Since the early 1990s, France has experienced four main substantial reforms of its first-pillar basic pension schemes. These took place in 1993, 2003, 2010 and 2014. In addition, several agreements between the social partners in second-pillar occupational schemes also took place, the last in 2017, which have also effected important changes. It should be noted that in 1995 the right-wing government of Alain Juppé was confronted by a massive public protest which forced it to drop planned moves towards a fully-funded third pillar scheme.

In a nutshell, the reforms to date have reduced the generosity of the first-two pillars of the French system in the following ways, by:

- increasing the length of the period of contributions needed to receive a full basic pension, from 150 quarters before 1993 to 172 quarters for the generation born in or after 1973;
- calculating the reference wage in the basic scheme on the best 10 years before 1993 and progressively extending the period to the best 25 years (by one year for each generation born between 1934 and 1948), truncated to the social security ceiling (whose level roughly amounts to the mean wage);
- indexing pensions (and wages for the reference wage) on CPI (Consumer Price Index) growth rate instead of nominal wage growth rate;
- increasing the minimum retirement age from 60 to 62 and the retirement age for full-rate pension from 65 to 67;
- decreasing the internal rate of return of the complementary schemes by raising the purchasing price of each point, thereby reducing the service value of each point; and, requiring extra contributions giving no points as well as temporary reductions in pensions in cases of early retirement.

As an illustration of these changes, we set out below how one specific generation has seen its rights evolve between 1992 and 2010, with no less than six different rules from ages 40 to 60 – including four reforms between the ages of 56 and 59.

Public spending in the French pension system (including complementary pay-as-you-go schemes) amounted to 13.8% of GDP in 2017. The average net pension of retirees living in France (including family bonuses and survivor's benefits) represented 65.3% of the average earnings of the working population. When all other sources of income are considered (homeowners' imputed rents excluded), the average living standard of retirees is 6% above that of the whole population and more or less equal to the level of employed people.

In 2015, the median living standard of retirees was equal to €1,770 per month. One retiree out of 10 had a living standard that was inferior to €1,090 (slightly above the poverty threshold). As a consequence, France has a relatively low level of poverty amongst retirees compared with other countries.

The net replacement rate over the lifecycle (defined as the ratio of the average pension during retirement to the average career earnings) is projected to decrease from 74% for a middle-class worker in the private sector born in 1940 to 60% for the same representative worker born in 2000 under the assumption of a 1.3% long term productivity growth rate.

## A SYSTEM WITH NESTED CONTRIBUTORY AND NON-CONTRIBUTORY BENEFITS

The French mandatory pension system provides a fairly good coverage of the population's needs at retirement, especially for low-to-middle income earners. Two elements contribute to this situation: the contributory component of the (defined benefit) basic scheme and of the (defined contribution) complementary schemes on the one hand, and the redistributive components of both schemes on the other.

Non-contributory elements are included in 'contributory' pensions: for instance, periods of unemployment are both included in contributory records for basic schemes and converted into points for complementary schemes. The same goes for illness, disability, and maternity periods. Credits are also available for parents who leave their jobs to educate their children and may be discounted for the purposes of calculating the reference wage under the *Régime général* rules.

Apart from these effects, inadequate contributory pensions can be complemented with a minimum pension (so called *minimum vieillesse*), which amounts (monthly) to €850 for single people or €1,300 for households.

The combination of contributory and non-contributory benefits makes it difficult to distinguish the proportion of pension benefits due to redistribution. The figure of 20% of pension expenditure (survivors' benefits excluded) due to non-contributory elements is frequently cited, as evaluated by the statistical department of the ministry of social affairs (DREES).

## COEXISTENCE OF NUMEROUS SCHEMES

In 2016, two-thirds of total pension payments were accounted for by pensions of wage-earners who had previously worked in the private sector (if one also includes the schemes for agricultural workers). Within these two-thirds, the point-based schemes were originally designed to generate a pension that was roughly half the size of the pensions paid by the basic schemes. For public servants, basic and complementary pensions are integrated and served by public schemes under the same rules, whether affiliates are working for the central state administration or with local and health institutions, even if the schemes differ somewhat in their financing. Many special schemes exist for salaried workers in specific public administrations (e.g. in energy and transportation), although this only represented 5% of total pension expenditure in 2016 (see table 4.1).

Table 4.1 Pension expenditures by schemes in 2016, in % of total expenditures

|  | *Schemes* | *% total expenditure* |
|---|---|---|
| Wage earners in private sector | CNAV: basic scheme for salaried workers in private sector | 37% |
|  | MSA: agricultural wage earners basic scheme | 2% |
|  | AGIRC ARRCO: complementary scheme for CNAV & MSA | 25% |
| Wage earners in public sector | Public servants of central administration | 17% |
|  | Public servants in hospital and local administration | 6% |
| Other workers | Complementary scheme for private workers in public sector | 1% |
|  | Agricultural self-employed | 3% |
|  | Other self-employed workers | 4% |
|  | Special schemes (energy, rail . . . ) | 5% |

Source: *Conseil d'orientation des retraites*, annual report, 2018.

The remainder of public pension spending is devoted to self-employed workers under different schemes linked to the specific nature of their work.

Information documents stemming from a pooling of the 35 main French schemes (among 42 known schemes) are available to affiliates reaching 35 years of age (for career duration information) or 55 years old (for information on expected benefits to come depending on the age of retirement).

If the current retirement regulations were to remain constant into the future, these proportions would change so that by 2070, CNAV would generate half of the expenditure (due to the growth of the private sector within the economy), AGIRC-ARRCO would remain at the same proportion (due to already scheduled decreasing returns) and other schemes would shrink from one-third to one-quarter of pension expenditure. Apart from the evolution of the population structure, the main drivers of these developments are to be found in the erosion of the defined-benefit properties of the schemes, as described below.

## A SYSTEM LOSING SOME OF ITS DEFINED BENEFIT PROPERTIES DUE TO BUDGETARY CONSTRAINTS

The reforms of the past two decades have relied on the three main levers to preserve the long-run sustainability of a pay-as-you-go pension system, namely: the level of contributions, the relative level of pensions and the retirement age (and/or the contribution record which is partly correlated with retirement age). Altogether, these reforms have weakened the defined benefit characteristic of the mandatory pension system and reduced its generosity[6].

*The reforms have helped meet the long-run equilibrium constraint* . . .

The 1993 reform has and will continue to have huge effects on the level of pensions as it switched indexation from a wage index to consumer price inflation and hardened the wage reference calculation for private sector schemes. Its effects – starting mainly for the cohort born in 1948 onwards – are evaluated to reach around five percentage points of GDP in the long run. The 2003 reform extended these rule changes to all schemes and increased the period of contribution required to obtain full rate pensions before the age of 65, for an effect evaluated at about two percentage points of GDP.

The 2010 reform (increasing the minimum and the full-rate retirement ages by two years) is estimated to reduce pension benefits more significantly in the short term than in the long run. In the long run, the reduced period of retirement is balanced by an increase in pension rights due to longer contribution records. The 2014 reform (which increases the required contribution record for a full-rate pension) has the opposite time profile: in the short term, the first generations hit by the reform only start to retire from 2030; in 2040, the 2014 reform generates an estimated reduction of pension benefits equivalent to 0.3 GDP percentage points (0.15 in 2030). Overall, when taking into account all the reforms adopted since

2010 (including complementary schemes) the reduction of pension benefits amounts to one percentage point of GDP per decade in the 2020s, 2030s and 2040s.

On the contribution side, the past reforms have increased both the legal retirement ages and the financial incentives to postpone retirement, generating more contributions to the schemes. Combined with the increase in contribution rates, the overall effect of reforms on levied contributions are evaluated at 0.6 GDP points in 2020, 2030 and 2040.

All in all, the financial balance of the pension system (excluding the public sector employees' schemes) is set to be improved by around 1.5% of GDP in 2040. In the shorter run, this improvement would mainly be due to the 2010 reform.

*. . . at the cost of eroding pension adequacy for future generations.*

The past reforms will also impact future retirees' living standards. Pension wealth (defined by OECD as "the size of the lump sum that would be needed to buy a flow of pension payments equivalent to that promised by the mandatory pension system"[7]) is a relevant indicator of pension adequacy both from an intergenerational and intragenerational viewpoint. It complements the replacement rate as a measure of the adequacy of pension benefits to meet beneficiaries' needs, since it takes into account the expected life expectancy at retirement and therefore the ability of mandatory schemes to cover the individual longevity risk.

## Effects of reforms within generations

For the generation born in or after 1980, the estimated pension wealth would be 4.5% lower following the reforms that have taken place. This evolution results from two opposite effects. On the one hand, pension benefits would be paid over a shorter timespan without reform (due to a higher effective retirement age), reducing pensions by 2.4%; on the other hand, the level of average pension with respect to average wage would increase by 2.1%.

The overall effects of past reforms are also expected to reduce the gender gap in pension wealth. Pension wealth would decrease by 6% for men born since1980, against 3% for women of the same generation.

Past reforms have undesired differential effects along the wage scale: the negative impact on pension wealth is heavier for low-wage earners (-7% for the first quartile of the distribution) than for high-wage earners (-3.4% for the fourth quartile).

## Effects of reforms between generations

When considering the four generations born in or after 1950, 1960, 1970 and 1980, it appears that the cumulated effects of all reforms have a stronger negative impact on the 1970 generation's pension wealth (-5.9%),with the 1950 generation being hardly affected (-1.2%).

Beyond pension wealth, other indicators may be used to assess the impact of pension reforms on retirees' well-being. Among them, the *Conseil d'orientation des retraites*[8] focuses on four complementary indicators, namely the length of retirement period (with respect to lifetime), the length of career, the average pension and the average contribution rate during career.

Despite the increase in life expectancy, the length of retirement with respect to lifetime would be globally stable for the generations born between 1950 and 1990, around 30% according to DREES[9]. The length of career with respect to lifetime would decline from 41.5% for the 1950 generation, to 39.8% for the 1990 generation.

The lifecycle replacement rate (defined as the average pension cumulated benefits received at retirement divided by the average cumulated earnings received during the career) would drop over the generations, from 55% for the 1950 generation to 45% for the 1990 generation (assuming a 1.5% long-term increase in labour productivity).

The impact of the pension reforms on lifetime contributory effort would also make the youngest generations the worst off: the lifetime contribution rate would rise from 23% for the 1950 generation to 27.8% for the 1990 generation.

## The cumulative effects of past reforms

The increase in the legal retirement age and the required contribution record for a full-rate pension are expected to improve the financial sustainability of the pension system in France.

The increase of the legal retirement ages has had a favourable impact on the employment rate of senior workers, but also on their unemployment rate. For the past 25 years, the employment rate of the 55–64 years old workers has been rising substantially as a consequence of an increase in female labour force participation and of the latest pension reforms. France, which had been lagging behind other OECD countries in terms of senior workers' employment, is progressively catching up, even if the specific role of pension reforms is difficult to isolate.

It may nevertheless have undesired side effects on other forms of public expenditure. The rigidity of labour markets in the short-run may impede older workers from staying in employment or finding a job should they become unemployed (due to their higher seniority-linked wages). In addition, an increasing desire on the part of older workers to remain in the workforce longer may cause negative externalities for younger workers, as some of the jobs that would otherwise have been vacated by those retiring will not become available. An increase in legal retirement ages may accordingly inflate unemployment or disability benefits. It has been assessed that, of the €14 billion reduction in pension benefits generated by the 2010 reform, 15% have in effect been replaced by an increase in disability benefits or social welfare benefits (unemployment benefits excluded)[10].

A difference-in-difference estimation between the first generations concerned by the 2010 reform (those born after 1st July 1951) and the previous ones suggests that the reform provoked a large

Table 4.2    How reforms have affected the 1953 generation

At age 39, affiliates born in 1953 needed a career of 37.5 years to be entitled to retire at 60 with a full pension. 20 years later, they have to face a lower reference wage (and lower rates of return in complementary schemes), as well as a longer period of contribution and a later retirement age. Changes have occurred abruptly, mainly impacting on those aged between 57 and 59, a few years before retirement.

| | reference wage | contributive record | minimal retirement age |
|---|---|---|---|
| age 39 (1992) | 10 best wages | 150 quarters | 60 |
| age 40 (1993) | | 160 quarters | |
| age 50 (2003) | | at least 164 quarters | 60 but 65 possible for long careers |
| age 57 (2010) | 25 best wages | | 61 |
| age 58 (2012) | | 165 quarters | 61 and 2 months |
| age 59 (2013) | | | 61 and 2 months but possible 60 for "long careers" |

Source: Conseil d'orientation des retraites.

increase in the employment rate at the age of 60, estimated at 24% for men and 22% for women. The probability of being effectively employed surged from 17% for men, and 16% for women. But underemployment also rose by seven percentage points for men, and six percentage points for women. The overall effect of the reform has been to extend the employment duration for those effectively employed to between 58 and 60 years old.

## THE CURRENT SYSTEM IS ASSESSED AS SUSTAINABLE IN THE LONG RUN AT THE COST OF A LOWER LEVEL OF PENSIONS RELATIVE TO WAGES AND OF A RISE IN THE RETIREMENT AGE

The Conseil d'orientation des retraites issued two reports in 2017[11] (the fourteenth such thematic report) and in 2018[12] that help to forecast the future of the retirement system under four economic scenarios, by pooling all retirement schemes results. These projection exercises are consistent with French demographic projections (to 2070) and the (short-run) economic forecast.

In the long run, pension expenditures show a great sensitivity to economic growth. Depending on the average real wage growth (1 to 1.8% per year), pensions might stay above 14% of GDP from 2035 to 2070 (at 1% growth) or drop below 12% of GDP (in case of 1.8% growth). This is due to the fact that pensions and reference wages are indexed against consumer price inflation: the higher the GDP growth rate, the greater the income gap in revenues between retirees and working people.

In line with the high sensitivity of pension expenditure to economic growth, the financial balance of the pension system (defined as the difference between overall contributions and overall public pension benefit, including survivors' benefits) also appears difficult to predict in the long run: the pension system could be in surplus or deficit from 2035, after a period of potential deficit between 2020 and 2035. The

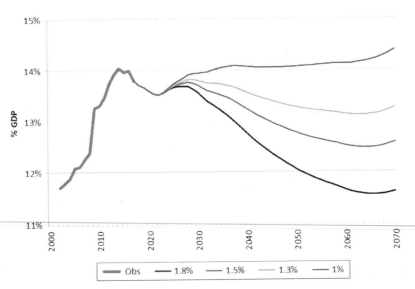

**Figure 4.1   Projected Public Pension Expenditure Under Four Real Wage Growth Scenarios (7% rate of unemployment).** *Source: Conseil d'orientation des retraites,* annual report, 2018. *Note:* 7% rate of unemployment from 2032 onwards.

price-indexing rules of pensions that disconnect the development of pensions and wages lead to an undesired uncertainty with respect to the future financial balance of the French pension system.

The *Conseil d'orientation des retraites* has assessed the contribution of three drivers that may contribute to balancing the public pension system in the long run: an increase in the retirement age, an increase in the contribution level and a decrease in the level of pensions with respect to wages. The effectiveness of these drivers depends on the different economic scenarios. From 2003 to 2070, the fall in the level of pensions relative to wages would always remain the main driver (covering from 41% to 69% of financing needs) while higher contributions would stay at a low 13 or 14% of financing needs (see figure 4.3). Higher constraints on insurance records or retirement age would meet 30% of the funding gap in any scenario.

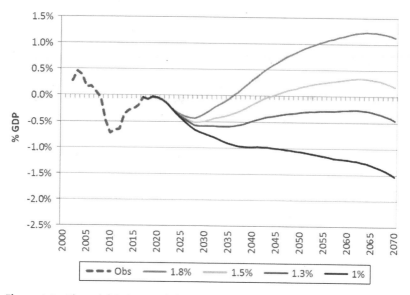

**Figure 4.2  Financial Balance of the French Public Pension System Under Four Real Wage Growth Scenarios (7% rate of unemployment).** *Source: Conseil d'orientation des retraites*, annual report, 2018. *Note*: 7% rate of unemployment from 2032 onwards.

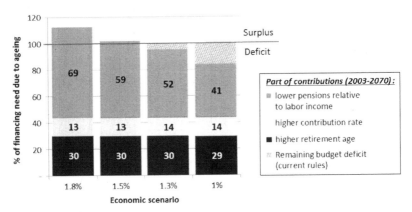

Figure 4.3 **The Contribution of Three Drivers to Meet Financing Needs Due to Ageing Between 2003 and 2070.** *Source: Conseil d'orientation des retraites,* annual report, 2018.

At the individual level, pensions relative to labour income are to fall among future generations of retirees, as illustrated by figure 4.4, even if the retirement age is expected to increase (figure 4.5).

Retirement would occur on average above 63.5 after 2035. It would be two years later than the most recent mean retirement age, and three years above 2010 retirement age. The change appears to have been accepted by the population, whereas this seemed unrealistic back in the late 1990s or early 2000s. It can be compared to the expected growth in life expectancy, where retirement length would always stay between 29 and 32% of total life span for all generations born between 1940 and 2000.

## THE VERY LOW LEVEL OF FUNDING IN THE FRENCH PENSION SYSTEM

Since the mandatory workplace pension schemes are mostly of a pay-as-you-go nature, there is little room left for funding in the French pension system.

Funding exists in some self-employed complementary schemes and in a small mandatory DC pension fund for civil servants.

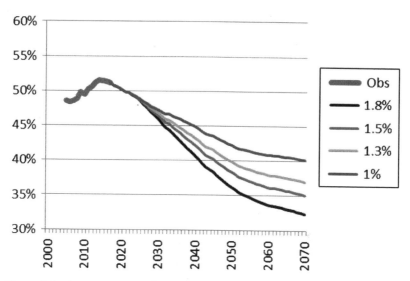

**Figure 4.4   Average Net Pension Relative to Average Net Labor Income.** *Source*: *Conseil d'orientation des retraites*, annual report, 2018. *Note*: Average result – not a replacement rate at individual level.

The second pillar AGIRC-ARRCO scheme also has accumulated reserves that represent 11 months of pension benefits. There is also a public pension reserve fund (*Fonds de réserve pour les retraites*) that has been created as a buffer fund for the first-pillar basic scheme. All these funds have accumulated reserves to limit the adverse

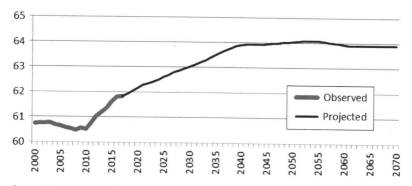

**Figure 4.5   Average Retirement Age.** *Source*: *Conseil d'orientation des retraites*, annual report, 2018.

consequences of the post-Second World War baby boom and of other shocks. These reserves represented less than 9% of GDP in 2016.

Employees can, if they wish, build up pension pots in voluntary occupational defined-benefit or defined-contribution pension schemes. Most (but not all), contributions are tax-exempted while pension drawdown is taxed. There are retirement savings products which can be accessed either through collective contracts (known as PERCO) or individual contracts (known as PERP). Designed by the 2003 reform to foster funding in the French retirement system, these products are also tax-incentivised.

On the whole, withdrawals from voluntary pension savings products represented only 2% of pension benefits paid to retirees in 2016. Only 12% of retirees benefit from an annuity paid out of a pension plan. The average annuity amounts to €2,250 per year, and the average yearly public pension to €16,700.

## WILL THE FUTURE REFORM CHANGE THE LEVEL OF FUNDING IN THE FRENCH PENSION SYSTEM?

The French Government has initiated a structural reform of the pension system whose main objectives are:

- simplifying the overall organisation of the system, by reducing the number of existing schemes;
- moving from a defined-benefit to a notional defined contribution system;
- immunising pension benefits from growth trends;
- improving intergenerational fairness;
- improving transitions between jobs; and
- (possibly) ensuring an automatic, instead of discretionary, monitoring of the system.

It is not possible, at the time of writing in Spring 2019, to predict the outcome of this re-organisation. If Swedish style notional defined contribution[13] is the model, retirees should become less concerned with career duration when deciding to retire (since every year worked increases entitlement), and more concerned by their replacement rate. As non-contributory benefits remain possible even under a defined-contribution system, it is unclear whether the future pension system will be more or less redistributive than it currently is. The detail will be key to assessing the advantages and drawbacks of such a reform.

The French Government has renewed its commitment to maintaining the pay-as-you-go pension system as the core of the social pact with no move towards a funded mandatory pension system. However, a step has been taken to reform the landscape of retail pension savings products, with the PACTE law presented at the Council of Ministers on 18th June 2018[14]. In a nutshell, the PACTE law will simplify and harmonise the rules applicable to pension savings products (e.g. relating to: age at drawdown; lump-sum payment, programmed withdrawals or annuity take up; portability; life-cycle default investment strategy; taxation). Three products will be available: one personal and two collective (one universal and one occupational dedicated to some targeted categories of employees). The Government expects to double the amount of contributions to retirement savings products within five years. This political targeting seems to be ambitious since pension coverage by the public pay-as-you-go pension schemes is still generous and the French household savings rate is fairly high. In fact, French households do cover their long-term consumption needs through the so-called 'life insurance contracts' (which are basically long-term savings contracts with high levels of tax incentive). It can thus be expected that French households will at best reallocate their savings towards these new products but are unlikely to significantly change their savings behaviour.

## NOTES

1. The French agricultural sector has a separate, but essentially identical, first-pillar system called the MSA (*mutualité sociale Agricole*).

2. *Association pour le régime de retraite complémentaire des salariés* (ARRCO) – association for the additional employee pension.

3. *Association générale des institutions de retraites des cadres* (AGIRC) – General association for executive pension institutions.

4. Social security for the self-employed.

5. Additional public sector pension.

6. This section draws on DREES (2016), « Les réformes des retraites de 2010 à 2015 », in Les dossiers de la DREES, December, n°9, 230 p. (in French).

7. OECD (2007) « Pensions at a glance: Public policies across OECD countries », p.40.

8. The *Conseil d'orientation des retraites* (Pensions Advisory Council) is an independent institution in charge of assessing the medium- and long-term prospects of the French pension system, both in terms of sustainability and pension adequacy. Its 40 members are representatives of social partner organisations, retiree associations, administrations, Parliament and qualified experts.

9. Direction de la Recherche, des Etudes, de l'Evaluation et des Statistiques – DREES (2016), « Les réformes des retraites de 2010 à 2015 », in *Les dossiers de la DREES*, December, n°9, 230 p.102.

10. Rochut and Rabaté (2017), "Employment and Substitution Effects of Raising the Statutory Eligibility Age in France", Paris School of Economics, working paper n° 2017–46.

11. Conseil d'orientation des retraites (2017) 14th Report (2017).

12. Conseil d'orientation des retraites Annual report (2018).

13. See McClymont and Tarrant, "Towards a new pensions settlement", Volume 1, (2016), p.59.

14. The PACTE law (*Plan d'Action pour la Croissance et la Transformation des Entreprises*) was set to be adopted by the Parliament during the last quarter of 2018.

# THE GERMAN PENSION SYSTEM

## Defined contribution begins

### Michael Schütze

In the German pensions system, the first pillar has dominated since Bismarck created the world's first contributory old age pensions system in 1889. Today, structural population change threatens its sustainability, however, and the government has reduced its value to the recipient. The replacement rate provided by the first pillar system has already fallen from 70% to 50%. The current government has agreed to aim for a replacement ratio of 48% over the long-term, which means that either the contributions of employers and employees need to rise, the pension age needs to be further increased, or another pillar must offer more retirement income. The first volume in this series discussed the 2001 *Riester* reforms which sought to bolster third pillar savings as a means of reducing the pressure on the first pillar, but which ran into controversy surrounding high and opaque costs and charges. This essay focuses on the German state's accompanying attempts both in 2001 and today in 2019, to strengthen the second pillar as a means to the same end.

## SECOND PILLAR PENSIONS

The second pillar in Germany has never reached the coverage levels of other developed countries. Around 55% of employees are now covered with a heavy bias towards those working in large companies and those with higher than average salaries. The system is sophisticated, or even complex, and has a long history, with the Bayer Pensionskasse for example being founded in 1897.

There are five types of second pillar provision in Germany. In 2016 the classical approach of a direct pension promise (*Direktzusage*) still accounted for around 50% of the German second pillar. The direct pension promise resulted traditionally in the creation of unfunded book reserves, although over the last thirty years a minority have gradually come to be funded on a voluntary basis. Second, insurance regulated Solvency I pension funds (*Pensionskassen*) account for 27% of the second pillar pension market. Third, regulated solvency II 'direct insurance' (*Direktversicherung*), a form of life insurance, accounts for 10.7%. Fourth, there is an older vehicle called a 'support' pension fund (*Unterstützungskasse*) which accounts for 6.3% of second pillar pensions; in its typical form today, this is a reinsured vehicle resembling direct insurance.

One way or another, all of these plans contain guarantees. Traditionally, as in historic defined benefit plans, they do so by guaranteeing a certain replacement ratio. More modern pension plans operate by guaranteeing returns on contributions that range from 6% down to 0%. Even the 'new kid on the block' – the fifth vehicle known as a *Pensionsfonds,* an insurance regulated, solvency I vehicle with more investment freedom and sometimes fewer actuarial restrictions – initially carried a capital guarantee, although these schemes were defined contribution in nature.

## 2001 PENSION REFORM 1.0 OR THE
## INTRODUCTION OF DC, GERMAN STYLE

The combination of contributions, demography and replacement ratio issues in a pay-as-you-go system was recognised 17 years ago and led to the first pension reform of 2001, as part of the Hartz IV reforms[1].

This represented a political compromise, which included:

- Employees received the right to save and create their own pension arrangements using tax-incentivised contributions of up to 4% of the social security ceiling.
- Employers could use external funding vehicles (i.e. *Pensionskasse*, *Pensionsfonds*, or direct insurance schemes) and thus dispense with providing capital and/or interest rate guarantees directly.
- The government freed the above mentioned 4% contributions from taxes and social security contributions.

These vehicles provided guarantees, the minimum being a capital guarantee on contributions to the end of the accumulation phase. In Germany this was dubbed 'defined contribution with a minimum benefit' (*Beitragszusage mit Mindestleistung*) – a DB/DC hybrid in the end.

In hindsight, there have been a number of success stories:

- Some industries have created their own industry-wide pension schemes, such as the metal and chemical sectors, although they still rely heavily on services from the insurance industry.
- Some employers have created their own 'Pensionsfonds'. The Bosch Pensionfonds AG was created in 2002 and by 2018 had accumulated assets of €6bn.
- A considerable number of employers and pre-existing industry-wide schemes have adjusted to fit their schemes within the new hybrid system.

The participation rate has risen substantially since 2001, from 14.6 million employees with a second pillar pension claim to 20.4 million by the end of 2015. Compared with the 36.5 million employees who have a claim in the first pillar pension system, general second pillar coverage is roughly 55%[2].

This certainly represents progress. However, looking at it from a different angle, while first-pillar pensions account for about 63%

of old age income, second pillar pensions still account for only 8%. This means, the ultimate goal of creating additional replacement pensions through the second and third pillars is still some way off, particularly when it is understood that the second pillar is confined largely to big companies and better paid employees.

## 2018 PENSION REFORM 2.0 OR THE INTRODUCTION OF DC WITHOUT GUARANTEES

The 2018 legislation is momentous in enabling the provision for the first time of pensions without guarantees. The objective is to expand coverage among smaller employers, for whom even a soft employer guarantee (returns on contributions) is deeply unattractive and among whom insolvency rates tend to be higher, which would potentially increase the strain on the German national pension protection fund (PSV aG). At the same time the longer period of lower interest rates has increased the risk associated with the conservative asset allocations which accompany necessarily guaranteed products. Very high allocations to fixed-incomes worked as long as there was a time- or term premium on interest-bearing instruments, which generated the returns needed to meet pension promises. With lower interest rates, pension promises can no longer be earned in this way. Contributions do not earn enough of a return to create sufficient replacement income, and sustainability demands greater allocations to risk premium assets, according to some sponsoring employers. In the last piece of the puzzle, the trade unions agreed to forfeit guarantees on future schemes if a decent tax-incentivised contribution rate was agreed and existing guaranteed provision was protected.

The result is a silent revolution, enabling a wide array of possible solutions and designs in the accumulation phase that can include the following features:

- DC plans that must result in a variable life annuity and with a prohibition of guarantees.

- Schemes delivered via any of the three insurance regulated second pillar vehicles.
- Schemes permitted only in conjunction with a so-called social partner model, which requires unions and employer associations to sign a labour agreement on a defined contribution pension plan, and requires them to participate on a permanent basis in the governance structure of the pension vehicle. In a similar way to the Dutch model, the expectation is that, at a minimum, a substantial number of social-partner driven pensions will be collective defined contribution pensions, and the social partners may define additional risk contributions, thus creating additional buffers.
- An increase of the tax-incentivisation of contributions from 4% to 8% which may, at least for income within the social security ceiling of €78,000, be sufficient to create a decent second-pillar pension replacement rate of between 60 and 70% in combination with the first pillar.
- The saving of social security contributions of up to 4% of the social security ceiling, and mandatory contribution of employers' savings on social security contributions into the social-partner DC plan.
- The opportunity to 'opt-out' altogether, which is one of the most prominent additional features to be included in the new legislation.

Regarding accumulation plans, while the choice of insurance-regulated vehicles and the prohibition of guarantees may lead to the assumption of a restricted range of solutions, there remain a number of options. Broadly categorised, there are now three possible ways to create an accumulation plan, namely through:

- Individual property rights, where any type of unit-linked, guarantee-free insurance solution and any derivation thereof may be used. This includes, life-cycle funds, target-date solutions for accumulation phase and even a system with individual retail fund choices similar to the US 401k system[3], although the latter is not what the legislator had in mind.

- Asset pool collectives, including the simple asset pooling of contributions to create economies of scale, broader and deeper diversification per participant and a reduction of costs, or an asset pool life-cycle, featuring various risk exposures within a single pool.
- Real collective systems, similar to the Dutch model. Here an investment collective for the accumulation phase may be created whereby investment risks may be shared between participants.

This is no 'retirement free-for-all' as in the UK, however, capital cannot be withdrawn and new DC plans must lead to a best estimate life annuity[4]. The pension vehicle is required to keep the scheme funding level in a range between 100% and 125%. When funding falls below 100%, pension payments must be cut, while when funding rises above 125% they must be raised. Buffers are also possible. Capital cannot be withdrawn by the individual at any time and a lifetime annuity must be calculated at retirement on the individual's behalf[5] – although there is the possibility of creating one large asset pool for savers and retirees with two separate risk sharing collectives, with one for accumulation and one for pensions.

Does the German system present too many possibilities? Our answer is 'no', as the task of unions and employers and their associations is to come up with solutions that fit the needs of individual companies and whole industries, and everything in between. This may of course also mean that the borders between the life insurance and asset management industries can become blurred.

The government has created a very wide and flexible framework for the German pension market which constitutes a big leap forward. Market participants now need to adapt to this new environment.

## NOTES

1. The Hartz reforms was a package of labour market adjustments that were part of the then government's Agenda 2010 reforms which sought to promote labour market participation. For a short assessment see

Odenhahl, C., (2017) "The Harz myth: a closer look at Germany's labour market reforms", Centre for European Reform.

2. Author's estimate. For a detailed breakdown of forecasts see Bundesminsiterium fuer Arbeit und Sozailes (November 2017) Pension Impacts Exercise.

3. For a discussion of the US system see Munnell, A.H.'s chapter on the United States in McClymont and Tarrant (eds) (2018) "Towards a new pension settlement), p.13.

4. There is a provision for trivial commutation (ie the withdrawal of pension contributions where only a very small pension pot has been built up).

5. There is also provision for the trivial commutation of lifetime annuities.

# THE GREEK PENSION SYSTEM AND THE ROLE OF DC SCHEMES IN RECENT REFORMS

## Olympia Mavrokosta

## INTRODUCTION

Greece's social security system has been an area of particular interest due to the significant recent reforms it has undergone. As issues of sustainability emerged, Greece, like most countries, has made extensive legislative and structural changes in order to reform its pension system. The introduction of defined DC pension plans represents a major redesign of pension benefits in the first and second pillar systems.

First-pillar contributions and benefits have undergone substantial modifications over the last decade, culminating in a drastic reform in 2016. For the first time, notional defined contribution schemes have been introduced into the first pillar, which previously consisted of defined benefit schemes only. The second pillar was also affected as legal provisions governing defined benefit schemes were amended to make them sustainable.

To explain the new role of DC plans, this chapter first presents a general outline of the first pillar's mandatory pension system, and then the voluntary schemes of the second pillar.

## THE MANDATORY SCHEMES OF THE FIRST PILLAR

Although all three pillars are provided in Greece's system, the vast majority of pensions are granted under the first pillar's umbrella; the first pillar is comprised of the main guaranteed income pensions and additional supplementary pensions.

Every person carrying out a professional activity subject to Greece's social security system is obliged to contribute to the main first-pillar pension. As a general rule, salaried persons contribute 6.67% of their salary and 13.33% is paid by the employer. A 13.33% contribution also applies to self-employed persons[1].

Currently, there are two kinds of obligatory supplementary pension schemes, the supplementary pension (designated as such), which provides an annuity only, and the separate lump-sum benefit scheme[2].Contributions for these pensions generally apply to salaried employees, while the self-employed are usually exempt. As regards annuities, the relevant percentage is set at 6%, and the contributions split equally between employees and employers, while lump sum contributions are set to 4% and are exclusively paid by employees.

Until recently, both main and supplementary pensions operated on a classical pay-as-you-go guaranteed income basis. While the main pension continues to be calculated on the basis of a guaranteed income system, supplementary pensions now operate on the basis of a notional DC (NDC) system first established in 2015.

The shift from DB plans to DC plans, even notional ones, was far from easy, due to the hostile public reaction to pension reforms. The NDC schemes were unpopular due to the absence of guarantees regarding the amount to be granted upon retirement. In times of economic recession, NDC plans usually lead to lower yields than those resulting from a DB plan. Against this background and taking into consideration the significance of supplementary pensions for individuals retirement income, it is not surprising that people remain skeptical about the introduction of NDC system.

## Main pensions

Maintaining a pay-as-you-go system operating on a DB basis was not a simple task for a country undergoing a serious economic depression. As is well known, pension expenditure in a pay-as-you-go system is mainly financed through social security contributions paid by employees and employers, and these fell substantially. Greece's working-retired ratio has also fallen from 1.7:1 in 2009 to 1.3:1 in 2017. Intense short-term pressures on the system have exacerbated longer term strains due to the increase in the life expectancy of the population and Greece's low birth rate.

Even before the financial crisis, Greece's pension provisions were subject to constant tinkering as part of an effort to ensure long-term sustainability[3]. Numerous attempts were made over previous decades to merge pension funds, increase the minimum pension age, and reduce pension benefits and replacement rates[4]. These amendments were often made by means of a fragmentary, sector-by-sector approach, outcomes varying dependent on the political pressure different professional groups were able to bring to bear in relation to their scheme[5]. Recently, however, under the Economic and Financial Adjustment Program, Greece's Parliament voted for a root-and-branch security social security reform. Some resulting measures, such those related to the new benefits calculation method, have since been implemented and the results are evident, while the effects of other measures remain to be seen.

A new pension law (4387/2016) became effective in May 2016. This law merged all the previously fragmented public social security funds into a single social security fund, called Ενιαίος Φορέας Κοινωνικής Ασφάλισης (E.F.K.A), or Unified Social Security Fund, operating under the same set of rules. New rules apply to every person subject to national social security legislation regardless of occupation, age or other factors, which had previously fragmented the system and allowed for unequal outcomes[6].

Under the reforms, pay-as-you-go guaranteed incomes were maintained for the main pensions, but new benefits calculations did strengthen the link between contributions and benefits. Structurally, the main pensions are now split into two parts: the state pension (non-contributory element) and the contributory element. The state pension is financed through taxes and has been set at€384.00 per month for the initial implementation of the new law, which corresponds to the relative poverty threshold in Greece. The contributory part depends on the years of insurance, contributions paid and replacement rates laid down in that law.

The aforementioned rules apply not only to pensions granted after the new law was adopted, but also to pensions granted under the previous rules. As a result, the latter pensions are being recalculated under the new rules, while maintaining some favourable provisions with due regard to acquired rights. Most importantly, the new laws do not lead to further cuts in pensions granted under the previous rules, which maintain the so-called "individual difference"[7].

## Supplementary pensions

The supplementary pensions of the first pillar have also undergone important changes. Funds have been merged, supplementary pensions have been frozen, and replacement rates have been reduced for accrued rights in funds with deficit. The introduction of an NDC system is, however, the most radical change regarding supplementary pensions.

The NDC applies to annuity and lump sum benefits, previously operating on a guaranteed basis. The selection of NDC rather than DC is easily understandable when considering implementation issues. The advantage to the state is that it enables the downward adjustment of benefits. Conversely, implementation of a funded DC system would have required the state to provide significant funds today, reflecting future retirees existing nominal pension contributions, and to forgo the use of their ongoing contributions to pay for current pensioners. A further advantage to the state is the mandatory nature of the NDC system of the first pillar. It means that employers and employees are obliged to participate and the contribution percentages are predetermined by law. Administrative costs are, therefore, relatively low and the number of members easily predictable.

In order for the shift to the NDC model to be smoother, it has only applied for contribution periods after 1st January 2015. While this makes the financial transition from one system to another relatively smooth, there are still many issues to be solved in order for the new system to be successful. First, there are practical issues regarding insured persons' data. Information needed in the context of a DB plan is not the same as that needed for a pension granted under a NDC plan. Some funds are currently collecting data related to paid contributions which are not in electronic form. In addition, the unfavourable economic environment and the fact that returns in an NDC system are based on performance of the national economy rather than assets invested in financial markets (including international ones) means that the pensions arising from the NDC model are not expected to increase considerably in the near future.

As a result, a debate recently reopened about alternative financial products that could play a role as a counterweight to steadily decreasing pension benefits in the first pillar. Occupational insurance is currently expanding, offering prospects for the development of pure DC plans operating outside the public pension system.

## SECOND PILLAR: VOLUNTARY OCCUPATIONAL SCHEMES

In Greece, pure DC schemes, so-called financial DC schemes, are those found outside the state pension and in the context of occupational insurance. Law 3029/2002 first established the possibility to offer such schemes as second pillar social protection. The legal framework governing the functioning of institutions for occupational retirement provision (IORPs) is as defined in EU Directives 2003/41 and Directive 2016/2341. In accordance with the implementing national legislation, IORPs take the form of private occupational pension funds, called Ταμεία Επαγγελματικής Ασφάλισης (T.E.A), or Occupational Insurance Institutions[8]. Use of such schemes is on a voluntary basis.

More specifically, occupational pension funds are established in the context of an occupational activity, by enterprise or sector of activity, at the initiative of employers or employees, or following an agreement between the two parties. Self-employed persons are also eligible to establish an occupational pension fund, individually or collectively. In all cases, a minimum number of 100 members is required for an authorisation to be granted.

Despite the fact that, according to the national legislation governing IORPs, there are no limitations related to the kind of schemes provided (DB or DC), all existing Greek IORPs are currently providing defined contribution plans without guarantees, following the international trend towards these schemes[9].

## The predominance of DC schemes in the second pillar

There are a number of reasons behind the predominance of DC schemes in the national second pillar. As stated above, the establishment of an IORP is voluntary and employers or employees have full freedom to participate or refrain. DC schemes provide significant flexibility regarding structure and monetary contributions.

The most important motive for establishing an IORP operating on a DC basis, however, is the fact that employers have lower liabilities compared to those arising from a DB plan (indeed, in most of the schemes established so far, no employer contributions are made). Nevertheless, some DC IORPs have been established by employees[10] or by employers and employees jointly. The regulatory costs associated with running a DB scheme in Greece are higher than those for a DC and this can make the latter attractive for smaller groups. In addition, under Greek law, a DC plan is potentially portable, allowing members to transfer the asset pot to a new scheme when changing employer or becoming self-employed. Employees may also consider flexibility around accessing benefits in retirement

to be attractive. The ability to select a spread of international investments in DC is also potentially attractive compared to an NDC system which links pension payments to local GDP growth.

## Issues and challenges

Since Greece lacks a specialised pension regulator with experience
of regulating private pensions, the national legislator opted for a
tripartite supervisory structure involving the relevant competent
authorities. National authorities designated to carry out the duties
provided in the respective legislation (hereinafter supervisory
authorities) are the following:

a)  the Ministry of Labour, Social Security and Social Solidarity
    (Υπουργείο Κοινωνικής Ασφάλισης και Κοινωνικής Αλληλεγγ
    ύης),
b)  the National Actuarial Authority (Εθνική Αναλογιστική Αρχή);
    and
c)  the Capital Market Commission (Επιτροπή Κεφαλαιαγοράς)

Supervisory authorities maintain distinct competences but cooper-
ate closely in order to monitor compliance with the relevant laws and
the protection of the interests of the insured persons. The schemes
themselves are run by management schemes which have a legal duty
to members first and they are required to operate on a not-for-profit
basis, unlike third pillar schemes run by insurers.

The Minister of Labour, Social Security and Social Solidarity may
take all appropriate measures, including administrative sanctions and
fines, to avoid or remedy any irregularities prejudicial to the interests
of insured persons. The National Actuarial Authority is empowered
with the monitoring of IORPs' economic functioning and sustainability regarding benefits and investment planning, playing an important
role for risk and solvency assessment. Finally, the Capital Market
Commission is empowered with supervising regulations related to
investments–a crucial element for the success of DC plans[11].

Currently there are 19 IORPs operating in Greece[12], 15 of which are voluntary and four are compulsory[13]. The latter were previously included under the first pillar but have transformed into private legal entities following law 4052/2012. In order to make use of that possibility, the four previously public funds had to transform into funded pension funds, adjusting their benefits accordingly. Participation in compulsory IORPs exempt their members from contributing to the NDC system of the first pillar. In this respect it should be pointed out that the four compulsory funds are the biggest occupational funds, in terms of assets, comprising more than 80% of the occupational pension market.

Converting from a mandatory, state-run public fund to a private pension fund was undoubtedly the first step towards the independence of supplementary pensions from the first pillar in Greece. Like the rest of the pension funds, the four compulsory funds opted for a DC scheme, following an agreement of both employers and employees.

Since the newly established funds still represent a relatively small share of the pension market, it is obvious that the second pillar is not yet an adequate supplement to the first. The second pillar's development is hampered by various factors. First, the institution of occupational insurance functioning under a funded system and on a voluntary basis was only introduced in 2002 and has not yet become part of the mainstream social insurance culture[14]. People have also been sceptical towards private pension funds, which have not been widely tested in practice[15]. Secondly, since IORPs operate DC schemes and most of them are still in the accumulation phase, it is not yet possible to assess the adequacy of benefits provided under those schemes.

Another important element to take into consideration is that participation in an occupational pension fund does not exonerate most potential participants from the obligation to pay contributions for main and supplementary pensions provided under the first pillar. DC schemes provide, of course, certain freedom as to the amount of money to be invested but contributing to such a fund still entails an additional financial burden that many employees cannot bear. As a result, occupational pension plans primarily serve insured people of middle or high-income, who, however, at this point tend to prefer to save in third-pillar pension products provided by established insurance companies.

## CONCLUSION

Greece has been taking important steps to redefine its pension system over the past decade. NDC and DC schemes are considered as a very promising part of the reform programme and are expected to do more to support the incomes of beneficiaries as the economy starts to grow. As in every case of newly introduced institutions, however, employer-based DC schemes need time to win public confidence. Economic depression has been a factor in slowing the take-up of the new workplace DC schemes. The reduction of average incomes over the austerity years has led to the reduction of savings, including pension savings. However, membership of such schemes had reached roughly 18,500 by the end of 2017 and is expected to grow further as new IORPs become established.

## NOTES

1. For further details, see Konstantinos Lanaras (2019), Insurance in EFKA, Sakkoulas.

2. For simplification reasons, both benefits will hereinafter be referred to as supplementary pensions.

3. For the effects of the recent economic crisis on greek social protection system, see Current issues of social protection law. Essays in honour of Konstantinos Kremalis, 2016, Nomiki Bibliothiki.

4. Relevant examples of these reforms are included in laws 1902/1990, 2084/1992, 3029/2002, 3371/2005, 3518/2006, 3863/2010 etc. For further details related to past reforms, see Angelos Stergiou & Theodoros Sakellaropoulos (2010), (eds.) *The Social Insurance Reform*, Athens, Dionicos.

5. Patrina Paparrigopoulou, Social Insurance Law, 2016.

6. Explanatory note of law 4387/2016.

7. Individual difference is the difference between the pensions paid to retirees who retired before 12 May 2016 and the pensions calculated under the new rules.

8. For further information on occupational insurance in Greece, see Patrina Paparrigopoulou, *Developments in Social Security Law*, Sakkoulas, 2004, Artemis Anagnostou-Dedouli, *Occupational Insurance in Greece*, DEN, vol.1503, November 2007 .

9. EIOPA, Report on market development, 2017.

10. Eg Institution for Occupational Retirement Provision of the Ministry of Finance.

11. Article 8 of Law 3029/2002.

12. Five more IORPs are expected to operate over the coming months.

13. 1) Occupational Insurance Fund of Insurers and Personnel of Insurers Companies (TEA-EAPAE), 2) Occupational Fund for Employees of Food Commerce 3) the Occupational Insurance Fund of Pharmaceutical Employees, 4) Occupational Supplementary Pension Fund of Personnel of Petrochemical Companies.

14. Petros Tsantilas, The establishment and the economic function of Occupational Insurance Institutions, EDKA, vol. MD', 2002, p. 890.

15. For a longer discussion, see eg Angelos Stergiou, *Occupational Pension Funds*, Overview of Labour Law, November 2016.

# THE INDONESIAN PENSION SYSTEM

## Steven Tanner

$P$ensions are at an early stage of development in Indonesia, although continued economic growth makes for enormous potential. This large and diverse archipelago nation has considerable natural advantages, not least in terms of human capital. Indonesia boasts the world's fourth largest population at over 250 million people, with a young demographic profile and is home to the world's largest Muslim population. Robust economic performance has seen a considerable decline in poverty and the rise of a middle class, with GDP per head up from US$807 in 2000 to US$3877 in 2018, according to the World Bank[1].

The country's sprawling geography comprises thousands of islands, although Java, with over half the country's population, is its economic and political heart. Formerly a Dutch colony, Indonesia gained its independence after World War II and has emerged since as a politically stable republic. Joko Widodo ("Jokowi"), elected president in 2014, won office on a wave of popular support and is the country's first president from outside the traditional elites.

The regulatory framework for both public and private pensions dates from 1992, with reforms to the public sector initiated from mid-2015.

## PILLAR I

The 1997–1998 Asian financial crisis was particularly damaging to the Indonesian economy, causing a contraction in economic output, a sharp rise in unemployment, currency devaluation and a fall in living standards. From that experience a national consensus developed to establish a universal and comprehensive social insurance scheme covering formal and informal sector workers.

A legal commitment for this undertaking was enacted initially in Law No 40/2004 concerning the Social Security Administrative Body – *Sistem Jaminan Sosial Nasional/SJSN*. This established the foundation for a reformed social insurance system with enhanced benefits to be introduced within a decade.

An implementation timetable followed in *Law 24/2011 concerning the Social Security Administrative Body – Badan Penyelenggara Jaminan Sosial*/the BPJS Law – and was enacted on 25 November 2011. This set out the merger of the four existing social insurance schemes serving certain working population groups into a single National Social Security System administered by a non-profit government agency (BPJS), with responsibilities divided between health (BPJS Health) and employment benefits (BPJS Employment), including pensions.

BPJS Health – *Badan Penyelenggara Jaminan Sosial Kesehatan* – launched on 1 January 2014 aimed to establish universal health cover for all Indonesians by 1st January 2019. BPJS Employment – *Badan Penyelenggara Jaminan Sosial Ketenagakerjaan* – was established from 1st July 2015 and administers all other social security benefits, including pensions.

Civil service employees (*PT Taspen*), the military (*PT Asabri*) and private sector employees (*PT Jamsostek*) have since been consolidated into BPJS Employment. The previous government social insurance agencies ran on a for-profit basis (*Persero*) stoking considerable scepticism among employers and members.

The ultimate goal of universal cover, however, has yet to be realised and despite reform, social insurance benefits mainly provide for the same specific occupational sub-groups, essentially public sector staff and formal private sector employees. The informal sector, which accounts for the greater part of the working population, may join on a voluntary basis, but membership is tiny.

A central reform initiative was enhancement to first-pillar pensions for eligible employees. Prior to their introduction, private sector employees were enrolled into a DC scheme through *PT Jamsostek* and required to contribute at a rate of 2%, with a further 3.7% paid by the employer. While this was a mandatory requirement, evasion among employers appears not to have been uncommon.

Accrued fund benefits under *Jamsostek* could be taken from 55, usually as a lump sum but a limited period payment benefit for up to five years was an option for larger sums. Annuities are in the market in a very modest way, with weak demand and little in the way of choice, and were mostly written mainly by a single state-owned provider. In practice, few *Jamsostek* members retained their benefits to retirement age with most taking benefit on early retirement with entitlement granted after five years.

In addition to DC benefits under *Jamsostek*, termination payments (severance) are a further mandatory requirement for employers under labour law, whereby employees are generally entitled to a lump sum on leaving service, with entitlement linked to length of service.

This framework meant the sum of *Jamsostek* and severance lump sum benefits in practice served more as short-term relief on leaving service, rather than a pension at retirement. Culture is an important item of note in Indonesia, and while there is a high propensity to save, the 1998 banking crisis left many with a cautious attitude towards entrusting their long-term savings to financial institutions.

While Jamsostek retirement benefit members are now absorbed into BPJS Employment, the DC scheme – *Jaminan Hari Tua* (JHT) – remains, and the contribution rate for employers and employees is unchanged. Rules regarding early benefit entitlement, however, have become a little more restrictive. Lump sum member benefits can only be taken at retirement, total permanent disability or emigration prior to retirement, though 10% of the fund balance is available to withdraw after ten years contributions and up to 30% is available for a home purchase.

In addition, social insurance reforms added a defined benefit scheme – *Jaminan Pensiun* (JP) – as a second-tier entitlement. This seeks to provide a secure retirement income, with pension linked to salary. JP membership is compulsory also for medium to large employers and may be phased in for smaller employers. The majority informal working population is not eligible to join but may join JHP on a voluntary basis.

With a minimum initial 15-year contribution period before being granted eligibility for benefits, the fund has a period to build assets to finance future benefits. This extensive lead time also means older cohorts are less likely to meet qualification minimums and will end up with a further lump sum benefit from this scheme too. JP also comes at an additional cost for employers and employers, an aggregate 3%, split 2% employer and 1% employee. Hence, total social insurance costs have increased from 5.7% to 8.7% of payroll for employers.

The level of projected salary-related pension income to qualifying members is expected to lie between a minimum IDR331,000 (US$24.17) and a maximum IDR3,971,400 (US$290.01) per month as of March 2018, with annual inflation adjustments. This compares with a minimum wage in Jakarta in 2018 of IDR3.65 million (US$266.54) per month. The DB accrual rate is 1% of average wages for each year of qualifying contributions.

Over the longer-term, this can be expected to provide more robust first-pillar provision. However, the low contribution rate under the JP scheme at just 3% is acknowledged to be inadequate in the long run for a DB scheme. Triennial increases of 0.3% or scheme redesign are possible options to underpin its sustainability. There is also a question as to how many members will meet the minimum service period requirements to qualify for pension income.

In acknowledgement of the long tail costs attaching to increasing life expectancy, the retirement age on both JP and JHT is raised to 56 years (from 55 previously). Under JP only, it increased to 57 from

1st January 2019 and subsequently by one year after every three years until it reaches 65 years as set out in Government Regulation No 45/2015.

BPJS Employment reported 8.2 million and 13.4 million members for the JP and JHT respectively in 2016, from a formal employed working population of 50.3 million. Informal members of the JHT, however, were a mere 47,651 from an informal working population of 70.3 million.

## PILLAR II

Supplementary employer-sponsored pension provision is voluntary and outside international employers and large domestic companies, remains relatively rare.

Workplace pensions first emerged in the early 1970s when a number of employers registered their pension funds with the Minister of Finance. Income tax legislation subsequently began to recognise registered pension funds and support them with tax concessions. Contributions to such funds became tax deductible and some investment income became tax exempt.

Private pension legislation enacted in 1992 (Law No 11/1992) promoted voluntary supplementary second and third-pillar provision, and established the Employer Pension Fund (EPF) and Financial Institution Pension Fund (FIPF) structures as permitted legal entities.

EPFs – *Dana Pensiun Pemberi Kerja* (DPPK) – are either DB or DC occupational pensions, with the majority (169 as of December 2017) being DB. They are designed for large employers and are more likely to be self-administered with investment management outsourced by mandate. The employees of more than one employer may be included provided all have access to equal benefits.

FIPFs – *Dana Pensiun Lembaga Keuangan* (DPLK) – are DC plans, marketed and administered by approved life insurers and banks. FIPFs are designed for the small and medium-sized enterprise

(SME), group and individual pension markets. There were 23 registered FIPFs in 2017 of which the majority are life insurance companies.

Market development has been slow with the number of registered pension funds contracting by more than a quarter since the early 2000s, from 321 registered pension funds in 2004, to 236 in 2017. Principally this is accounted for by the demise of defined benefit (DB) provision since 2002, though they still account for over 70% of total registered funds. Registered occupational defined contribution (DC) schemes, making up the balance, have risen marginally in number in recent years.

Membership, however, has increased slowly albeit from a low base. The Financial Services Authority – *Otoritas Jasa Keuangan* (OJK) – reported 4.39 million supplementary pension members, a penetration rate among eligible workers of 6.26% in 2016.

There is some support for second-pillar provision through the tax system but trade union support is less pronounced.

Second-pillar development has been checked in recent years by social insurance reforms long in the making, which have forced higher costs on employers from 1st July 2015 and promise enhanced benefits to covered employees. While this has brought clarity, it has done little to encourage further voluntary second-pillar provision with employer contribution costs increasing by an initial 2% of payroll and employees' by 1% of salary following the addition of the JP defined benefit social insurance scheme. Employers are wary also of JP contribution increases in future.

Second-pillar DB plan benefit is based generally on a maximum member pension of 80% of final pensionable salary. In most instances the actual benefit is between 50% and 60% of final pensionable salary. Pension increases are subject to individual scheme rules.

DC plan benefits are the accumulated fund value at retirement. Pension annuities purchased at retirement are subject to the relevant terms and conditions under the selected annuity.

In the long-term, the prospects look bright for private pensions as growing affluence expands the consumer class and awareness and demand for pensions gradually take hold. The addition of a regulatory framework for sharia-compliant pensions from September 2016 may, in time, further encourage market development.

FIPF membership has risen 55% in the five years to 2016, DB EPF membership meanwhile has remained flat over the same period.

## PILLAR III

Long-term life insurance savings policies have traditionally been marketed as third-pillar retirement savings plans and it was not until the 1992 legislation that a legal framework for individual private pensions was established. The DC-based FIPF can provide for both groups and individuals.

Third-pillar need is greatest among the largely uninsured informal working population comprising the majority of workers, reported to total 70.3 million in 2015. This group, however, is generally low paid, often living at the subsistence level, not financially literate and hard to reach. A mere 47,651 joined the social insurance retirement savings plan (JKN) by the end of 2016.

In spite of these challenges, individual FIPF membership continues to report steady progress in a niche market. The OJK reported 841,170 individual active FIPF policies in 2016 – a 5.1% increase over the previous year. The buyer profile of individual policyholders is not reported but their appeal is likely to be attractive to successful entrepreneurs, affluent individuals without pension provision and potentially some longer-term expatriates.

FIPF pensions, both individual and group, are marketed and sold by licensed financial institutions, of which 23 were registered with the OJK as of December 2017. The majority of these were life insurance companies and the rest are banks, although the market leader in the sector is the state-owned bank, BNI (Persero) Tbk.

## NOTE

1. World Bank (2019) Indonesia Overview.

# SWITZERLAND

## The pension system

## Benita von Lindeiner and Ueli Mettler

## INTRODUCTION

Much as Swiss German is difficult for people in other German-speaking countries to understand, the Swiss occupational benefit system is also rather difficult to grasp from the outside. Even a simple attribution of a pension plan as defined benefit or defined contribution under International Financial Reporting Standards (IFRS) accounting standards is tricky as Swiss plans share features of both. This chapter will shed some light on the often misunderstood Swiss system of occupational benefits, which manages to align interests of the different parties remarkably well while reducing informational asymmetries by enforcing a high degree of transparency. There remain important challenges for the future, however, as Switzerland is a direct democracy and the last two attempts at necessary reforms to make the system more sustainable have failed at the ballot box.

## THE SWISS THREE PILLAR SYSTEM

Switzerland's system of retirement provision is broadly based on three pillars that are enshrined in article 111 of the Swiss

Constitution. The first pillar, the Federal Old-Age, Survivors' and Disability Insurance (OASI/DI), was introduced in 1925 to cover basic subsistence needs in old age and costs arising in the event of death or disability. The second pillar, Occupational Old-Age, Survivors' and Disability Insurance, has a long-standing history and was made compulsory in 1985, aiming to ensure the maintenance of an adequate standard of living in retirement. At the time of introduction, over 80% of all Swiss employees were already covered by voluntary occupational benefit schemes. The first and the second pillar are designed to jointly provide old-age provisions of approximately 60% of the last salary. The third pillar, a restricted voluntary insurance scheme, was incorporated into the constitution in 1972: the federal government and the cantons encourage private pension schemes aiming at the maintenance of the former standard of living.

While the first pillar of basic insurance is a pay-as-you-go system and is in general mandatory for each person living or working in Switzerland, the second pillar, the occupational retirement scheme, is funded and covers all persons in gainful employment with an annual wage exceeding a minimum threshold. The third pillar is purely voluntary, offering tax incentives and promoting property ownership.

The Swiss first pillar faces the same problems confronting other pay-as-you-go systems throughout the industrialized world due to an increasing dependency ratio, low birth rates and rising life expectancy. The third pillar acts as a savings system and can be utilized according to individual requirements. The most remarkable feature in the Swiss system of retirement provision, however, is its occupational benefit scheme, the second pillar. This reached a total size of CHF906 billion (US$910 billion), including vested benefit accounts, or 133.1% of GDP in 2017. It still works remarkably well, despite a pronounced need for structural reforms.

## THE SWISS SECOND PILLAR

All workers in Switzerland covered by the first pillar OASI/DI and in receipt of an annual salary of more than CHF21,150 must be covered by an occupational pension scheme in the second pillar. The employer is obliged to either establish a pension institution or seek association with one. The occupational benefit institutions are non-profit organizations, they provide old age and disability insurance and must be jointly managed by employees and the employer. They are responsible for collecting savings during the accumulation phase and – less commonly internationally – for directly paying out pensions in the decumulation phase.

In the accumulation phase, each actively insured person has an individual account at her employer's benefit institution with her accumulated savings. A change of employer results in the full transfer of the accumulated assets plus accrued interest from the benefit institution of the former employer to the benefit institution of the new employer, irrespective of the benefit institution's funding ratio.

At retirement, each insured person can choose between receiving a lifelong pension or a partial or total lump-sum payment of her retirement assets. The retirement assets are equal to the sum of all contributions plus accrued interest, again irrespective of the benefit institution's funding ratio and thus subject to very limited financial market risk. The level of the pension is determined by the conversion rate, which represents the proportion of retirement assets that will irrevocably be paid out per annum for the remainder of the pensioner's life. After death, entitled spouses receive a predefined fraction of the deceased's pension for the remainder of their lives.

Benefit institutions can be either exclusive per employer and affiliated companies or open to multiple employers as collective benefit institutions – a structure increasingly gaining importance for smaller companies in recent years.

## THE SETUP UP OF OCCUPATIONAL BENEFIT INSTITUTIONS

All occupational benefit institutions are subject to cantonal and federal regulatory authorities and must be entered in a register according to Art. 48 BVG/LPP. There is a substitute pension fund for those employees not covered under the scheme, for unemployed and for the voluntarily insured self-employed. If a benefit institution runs into severe financial difficulties, consists of mostly pensioners or has been liquidated, a Guarantee Fund that is jointly financed by all pension funds through mandatory contributions ensures that all obligations are met.

All Swiss benefit institutions are independent of the employer; their highest governing body always consists of both employee and employer representatives. Most benefit institutions are set up as foundations and governed by a board of trustees with far-reaching responsibilities and legally-defined duties. It decides (1) on the organisational setup; (2) the organisation of the investment activities; and (3) the choice of the type of provision.

Decisions on the organisational setup include basic choices of the funding type as a defined benefit or a defined contributions scheme – with the latter gaining ground as the share of DB plans dropped to only 5.3% in 2017 among private-sector benefit institutions with no federal guarantee, according to the most recent survey of Independent Regulatory Commission (OAK BV/CHS PP) in May 2018. It is also necessary to decide between independent setup and affiliation with a collective benefit institution, as well as on the benefit scheme and valuation, the selection of an executive manager and the selection of an accredited pension fund actuary (Art. 51a BVG/LPP).

Setting up investment activities necessitates extensive decisions on investment strategy, which must be suitable for the benefit institution's risk-bearing capacity and which must ensure the medium- to long-term accordance of assets and liabilities. The investment process of the entire actuarial capital is also the sole responsibility of the board of trustees in terms of defining goals, managing execution and monitoring any mandated asset manager.

Finally, the board of trustees needs to decide on the insurance concept: autonomous foundations carry the risks of invalidity, death and financial risk independently. Semi-autonomous foundations enter into reinsurance contracts to cover the risks of death and disability of the actively insured, while fully reinsured foundations delegate even financial market risks to a large extent to insurance companies who take over the payment of life annuities.

Each benefit institution must disclose its balance sheet, profit and loss account and detailed additional information on its governing bodies, development, administration and asset management in an audited annual report. All statutes by which the board of trustees determines benefits, reserves, organisational matters, asset management and any partial liquidations must conform to federal law and be approved by cantonal regulatory authorities.

## LEGAL GUARANTEES

While there are many degrees of freedom for the board of trustees or other governing body, there are also very strict minimum requirements, or guarantees, that are binding for all occupational benefit institutions in Switzerland. All guarantees, however, apply to so-called "mandatory coverage" only. This is the hypothetical amount of retirement assets that employees would have accumulated if the pension fund had collected nothing but the legally defined minimum age-dependent saving contributions on annual wages between CHF21,150 and CHF84,600. Contributions start at 7% of the insured wage – equally shared between employer and employee – at the age of 25, and finally rise to 18% for all employees aged 55 and older. The vast majority of Swiss benefit institutions, however, voluntarily stipulate higher savings rates – of which the employer again needs to provide at least 50%. Any assets accumulated in excess of the mandatory coverage are called extra-mandatory coverage and are not covered by any legal guarantees.

### Minimum interest rate

Investment performance is not directly related to the development of the retirement assets, as a capital guarantee is in place. Rather, according to Art. 15 para. 2 BVG/LPP, retirement assets must bear interest at a minimum rate fixed ex-ante by the Swiss Federal Council and reviewed at least every other year. For 2018, the minimum rate lies at 1.0%. Rates below that level need to be justified by an overall poor financial condition of the benefit institution; deviations above that level lie at the discretion of the board of trustees. In 2017, when financial markets showed a stellar performance and the average pension fund in Switzerland, measured by the Credit Suisse Pension Fund Index, achieved 8.05%, the average interest rate granted among benefit institutions with no federal guarantee was 1.95%. This stands in stark contrast to the current 10-year Swiss government bond yield, which reached -0.01% in July 2018. Although the minimum interest rate theoretically applies to the mandatory share of the retirement assets only and the board of trustees is free to grant interest on the extra-mandatory coverage at its discretion, most benefit institutions stick to a single interest rate.

## Minimum conversion rate

In addition to the minimum interest rate, which provides a guarantee for the actively insured, there are also guarantees for retirees and pensioners. Art. 14 para. 2 BVG/LPP, stipulates a binding minimum level for pension payments by defining a minimum conversion rate at which the assets accumulated within the mandatory coverage levels must be converted into an annual pension. This minimum conversion rate currently lies at 6.8%, a rate which is, in view of the present life-expectancy, equivalent to an implicit annual interest rate of approximately 4.8%.

There are no legal constraints for the board of trustees when determining the conversion rate on the assets accumulated above the mandatory coverage levels. Given the current interest rate environment with risk-free rates around zero, benefit institutions need to rely on the above-mandatory coverage to reduce average conversion rates to sustainable levels. However, it must be born in mind first that the minimum threshold is always binding (see above), and pension payments must not fall below the amount arising from the minimum conversion rate and the mandatory coverage level, and second, that a too low conversion rate entices high lump-sum withdrawals at retirement.

The minimum conversion rate on the mandatory coverage level is not the only guarantee enjoyed by Swiss pensioners. Most importantly, once a pension is taken it is unalterable. This guarantee works irrespective of financial market turbulence, economic crises or the liquidation of the employer, and it applies to the total pension, not just to the legal minimum. Furthermore, it is valid for the entire remaining life of the pensioner and potentially of any surviving spouse or dependent children, who will, if entitled, receive a share of the deceased's pension as defined by the board of trustees in the pension fund's statutes. Together with the minimum guarantees, these features cause Swiss DC plans to be classified as DB plans according to IFRS – despite the fact that there is no right of recourse to the employer and that Swiss benefit institutions are legally independent entities. At the same time, these constraints allow for a high degree of security for the entire insured population.

## Costs of the guarantees

Given interest rates at or below zero, it is obvious that the system cannot be financed at risk-free rates as these guarantees are very costly. Even the average conversion rate of benefit institutions with no federal guarantee – i.e. the conversion rate on the mandatory and on the above-mandatory coverage – currently lies at 5.5%, equivalent to an interest rate guarantee around 3.0%. In addition, the minimum interest rate on retirement assets, currently 1.0%, cannot be financed by relying solely on risk-free Swiss government bonds, and constantly increasing life expectancy adds pressure to the system. To finance benefits as required by law, Swiss benefit institutions need to be able to bear considerable amounts of investment risk.

## Risk-bearing capacity

The Swiss second pillar, however, is set up to provide considerable risk-bearing capacity which arises from three pivotal conditions that form a crucial part of the setup:

1. Not-for-profit structure: benefit institutions within the second pillar are non-profit organizations. The risk is jointly carried by a "solidarity community" consisting of employees and the employer. This setup generally ensures alignment of interests. A profit-oriented risk-bearer probably would not be willing to take over the corresponding financial market risk.
2. Compulsory insurance: the pension system is mandatory for all employees with an annual salary above CHF21,500. Without this obligation, individuals might decide to withdraw their money during a financial crisis or a shortfall in coverage.
3. No free pension choice: employees cannot freely choose their benefit institution but are collectively bound to their employer's institution.

This setup – in particular the compulsory nature of the insurance and the commitment to the employer's benefit institution – allows for an intertemporal risk transfer. Swiss benefit institutions can deal with temporarily negative or low returns on financial markets as they are able to endure temporary underfunding without risking a loss of insured individuals. Rather, the setup allows them to transfer low financial market returns to future generations enjoying high financial market returns. Just as certain generations, however, profit from the guarantees that pension funds provide in case of financial turmoil, they are also required to contribute to the benefit institution's funding ratio when financial markets rally by accepting benefits below that level.

The great advantage of this intertemporal risk transfer lies in the possibility to smooth financial market risks over generations. Consequently, the sum of risk tolerance over all generations is significantly above the risk tolerance of a single generation, as Allen & Gale formulated in 1997. Accordingly, the intertemporal risk transfer results in a higher risk-bearing capacity and a higher expected performance of the collective insurance scheme as opposed to individual pension schemes.

This setup thus makes it possible to take significantly more financial market risk than a private insurer ever could. Depending on the structure of the insured population and the employer's overall situation, benefit institutions can rely to a higher or to a lesser degree on the risk transfer – and accordingly invest in risky assets. Benefit institutions consisting only of pensioners must invest on a risk-free basis, however.

The regulatory framework of the Swiss second pillar also provides for sustainability measures: first, a benefit institution may introduce recovery measures in case of financial difficulties if a rebound within the next 7–10 years cannot be expected. The employer must carry at least half of the burden of these measures. Second, the Guarantee Fund steps in if a recovery does not seem achievable. This is especially important in cases in which the bankruptcy of the employer – which removes the fundament of the intertemporal risk transfer – coincides with an underfunding of the benefit institution.

## CHALLENGES IN THE FUTURE

The greatest challenge the Swiss second pillar faces in the near future is the cost of guarantees, especially of the minimum conversion rate. Both an implicit interest rate of 4.8% on the mandatory coverage or even an implicit interest rate around 3.0% on average are unsupportable. They currently require a constant cross-subsidisation from the actively insured – in terms of interest significantly below market returns – to new pensioners. The last two attempts to reduce the minimum conversion rate – in 2010 and in 2017 – failed at the ballot box; it is indeed difficult to obtain approval of the sovereign electorate to reduce future pensions.

Another great challenge lies in the gradual rise of collective benefit institutions. An increasing number of pension funds have decided over the last year to join collective benefit institutions in order to handle increasing administrative complexity and legal obligations. They are free, however, to terminate their affiliation, attractive if the collective benefit institution runs into financial difficulties. This, however, seriously jeopardizes the intertemporal risk transfer and thus seriously hampers the risk-bearing capacity. Clear rules with respect to the handling of reserves and free resources are necessary to ensure that this development does not run against the foundation of the Swiss second pillar.

## GOOD GOVERNANCE AND TRANSPARENCY OF THE SWISS SYSTEM

The Swiss second pillar applies – with its strict regulations – a relatively high degree of coercion on the insured population, which indisputably requires powerful governance regulations. The most important corporate governance element in the second pillar is without a doubt the equal composition of the board of trustees as the highest governing body. The trustee system in general allows for an alignment of interests that private insurance providers with shareholders focussed on profit maximisation cannot possibly achieve. In addition, the equal composition of the governing body with employer and employee representatives strengthens the alignment of interests by equipping both parties with equal power.

However, the tasks and the legal obligations that a board of trustees faces are multifaceted and plentiful. This stands in stark contrast to the fact that the board usually works on a voluntary basis with little to no compensation and additional regular occupational duties. Consequently, the board needs to delegate a significant amount of its tasks to other internal or external organs. Specifically, the board requires the assistance of an executive administration and often of a management team, of investment professionals, of reinsurance companies and of actuarial experts and investment consultants to fulfil its legal duties.

Delegation of power, however, gives rise to principal-agent conflicts as information tends to be asymmetrically distributed. Furthermore, a lack of transparency increases the potentially harmful nature of informational asymmetries at the detriment of the less informed party, ie the insured population, and reduces the overall confidence in the system itself. This became very evident in the 2010 attempt to reform the Swiss second pillar, which was rejected due to the general sentiment that asset managers were actually "stealing" pension money and that asset management costs were not truthfully disclosed.

A structural reform that was introduced in 2011 aimed at improving governance regulations and at greatly increasing transparency on both sides of the balance sheet. Today, principal-agent problems in delegation are mitigated by the following legal measures:

a)  Separation of power: most importantly, the law and the regulations focus on preventing conflicts of interest. Members of the highest governing body are barred from all involvement in the pension fund's executive board and from the asset management of the actuarial capital. This separation of power also applies to the actuary reviewing the benefit institution.

b)  Transparency requirements: very far reaching transparency requirements have been established to prevent informational asymmetry and to strengthen the overall trust in the system. Anyone mandated with the executive management, administration or asset management of a benefit institution must specify the form and the level of compensation in an unambiguous, written contract. This also applies to asset managers with respect to retrocessions (kickbacks, trailer, or finders' fees), which need to be disclosed and handed over to the benefit institution. In case of transactions with related parties, competitive offerings must be obtained, and the assignment must be made fully transparent. Finally, all insurance companies offering solutions to the Swiss second pillar must disclose their BVG-related profit-and-loss accounts separately and face a limit on the income potentially distributed to shareholders.

Since the structural reform, Switzerland also has one of the most transparent regulations with respect to asset management costs. Based on a comprehensive TER-TTC-SC (total expense ratio, transaction costs and tax and supplementary costs) concept, all asset management costs must be published in the annual reports of the individual benefit institutions and cannot be directly offset against investment returns. Specifically, asset managers are forced to publish officially accepted TER ratios on all investments[1], including collective investment vehicles and fund-of-fund structures. Asset managers that fail to provide transparent TER ratios will see their products listed in the annex of the annual report in a list of all non-transparent investment vehicles. This annex serves as a blacklist, the threat of which has indeed encouraged almost all asset managers to comply since the introduction of the requirement in 2013.

c)  Personal liability: finally, the Swiss regulations have indeed managed to install the 'prudent man' rule with respect to the board of trustees by enforcing personal liability, thus ensuring the board takes responsibility for its decisions. The concept is backed by a ground-breaking ruling of the Swiss Federal Supreme Court published in December 2017 (decision 9C_752/2015) with respect to the Provitas collective benefit institution. Provitas' obligations had been taken over by the Guarantee Fund in 2002 after a decline in the funding ratio to 71%, resulting in charges against the board of trustees for choosing an overly aggressive investment strategy and not monitoring the mandated asset manager diligently enough. The confirmation of the personal liability of the board of trustees by the Federal Supreme Court will clearly contribute to prudent person behaviour and will prevent the board from investing assets too aggressively, relying on the Guarantee Fund in case markets do not perform.

## CONCLUSION

The Swiss second pillar is generally regarded as a great success story. Based on the funding principle, it covers 81.6% of all employed persons in Switzerland (2016) and helps – together with the first pillar – to raise replacement rates to 60% of the final insured salary, allowing the working population to, on the whole, feel relatively relaxed about the future. The minimum guarantees that the system provides irrespective of financial market performance allow for a very high degree of planning security for old age. They can be afforded due to the unique setup of the system that allows for intertemporal risk transfer and thus enjoys a higher risk-bearing capacity than individual insurance ever could by itself.

The success of the system, however, critically hinges on rather detailed governance and transparency regulations. The trustee-system ensures the general alignment of interest; the personal liability of the board of trustees helps to implement the prudent man concept. Far-reaching transparency regulations both with respect to the management of the benefit institution as well as the asset management itself help to alleviate problems arising from asymmetrically distributed information and enable the board of trustees to delegate some tasks while mitigating principal-agent problems. Court rulings regarding personal liability and transparency of all forms of compensation have successfully enforced these rules.

There remain important challenges, however. Most importantly, the current level of benefits that the system provides due to the minimum guarantees is too high. In light of rising life expectancy and record low interest rates, it can only be financed by accepting constant cross-subsidisation from the actively insured to new pensioners, threatening to exhaust those solidarities that the system was originally built on. Future pensions will need to be reduced, but it has proved extremely difficult to get the Swiss sovereign electorate to agree to these measures. Furthermore, the rise of collective benefit institutions that allow affiliated individual benefit institutions to cancel their contracts undermines one of the core pillars of the intertemporal risk transfer, thus seriously jeopardising the *raison d'être* of the Swiss second pillar. A comprehensive, clear and targeted regulation of collective benefit institutions still needs to be established.

## NOTE

1. The TER is a more comprehensive account of the costs incurred in managing a fund than the annual management charge because fees for a range of services including legal, administration, audit, marketing, directors, and regulatory costs. It does not however include transaction costs.

# UK

## *First steps in allowing collective DC*

## Kevin Wesbroom

In 2016, the chapter covering the UK in the first volume of this series, stated: "The UK is in the midst of major reform of pensions"[1]. The chapter went on to cover the roll-out of auto-enrolment, the inexorable growth of DC as the pension solution, and the 'freedom and choice agenda'. It also observed that, when asked, savers said they wanted "pension provision that supports members' best interests without requiring active member choice"[2]. In March 2019 the UK government responsed positively to its consultation into another potential major reform of UK pensions[3] which firmly and squarely addresses this requirement – namely, the introduction of collective defined contribution (CDC) schemes.

The government's response to this consultation makes it clear that the UK version of CDC will be different from those in other jurisdictions, such as the Netherlands and some Canadian provinces, but the UK will learn from their CDC experiences. The UK will not convert past pension entitlements into CDC benefits. This changes the balance between generating higher returns and benefits, and protecting those benefits, and specifically shields members from cuts in existing DB pensions.

The fundamental nature of CDC is that benefits are not guaranteed. Guarantees cost, in terms of the investments needed to deliver those guarantees, potentially lowering the eventual income available from the same level of pension saving[4]. CDC frees a scheme from these guarantees, opening up the prospect for investments that generate higher returns, and hence higher expected benefits for members – albeit at the price of there being a higher chance of having to make pension adjustments in the future.

The vision painted of the UK CDC system is not one that incorporates the multiple layers of prudence that are associated with CDC schemes elsewhere, including in Germany as applied to the retirement phase. As discussed elsewhere in the volume, this can also include prudence by the actuary, in terms of the choice of assumptions used to place a value on future liabilities, followed by explicit buffers or reserves needed before benefits can be adjusted. This approach can make eminent sense where past benefits have been converted from defined benefit to CDC but is not needed when the CDC scheme is starting from scratch and past benefits are left unadjusted. The UK system envisages 'best estimate' actuarial assumptions about future returns and other demographic issues, notably longevity, and no explicit buffers before benefits are adjusted. Buffers and prudence mean withholding benefits from one generation and distributing them at a later stage, which requires the exercise of significant judgement and which can increase the chances of intergenerational unfairness.

Taking away buffers and prudence might lead to concerns that benefits will be inherently volatile, and much closer to conventional DC with none of the 'smoothing' that is associated with CDC concepts. This will not be the case if the CDC model adopted is similar to that proposed by Royal Mail, which has been a driving force behind the renewed interest in CDC in the UK. Royal Mail's proposed plan uses future increases to benefits as the implicit buffer that is used to smooth out market volatilities, thus offering members more stable benefits.

Under this approach, an annual actuarial valuation would be carried out, using the best estimate assumptions noted above to value liabilities. The valuation would 'solve' the following question: what sustainable level of future increases in benefits can be supported by the market value of a scheme's assets? That level of sustainable increase would then be granted to members for that year. The benefits that are targeted would incorporate 'inflation proofing', all the way from the date of any award to the date the benefits are paid, followed by indexation in payment. The value of an inflation proofed pension is significantly higher – perhaps double in value – compared with a 'flat' benefit which carries no such increases. The difference provides the buffer to protect members from cuts in pensions, and the mechanism for smoothing benefits from year to year. We might start from a position where the sustainable level of increase is in line with inflation – say 3% per annum, but we might then experience a 20% drop in market values. The next annual actuarial valuation could then show that the sustainable level of increases had reduced by 1% per annum, bearing in mind the fact that those inflation increases apply over a prolonged period of time. The actual annual increase granted to members would then be the lower sustainable figure of 2%, compared with 3% the previous year. A severe market drop becomes a somewhat lower rate of annual increase in benefits which is a form of smoothing, but one that does not require a judgement call by trustees or other scheme advisers that markets are 'too high' or 'too low' or some such.

The effect of a full market drop would however be experienced by a member who wishes to transfer out of the CDC scheme. Transfer values – which would be available up the point that benefits become payable – would reflect an equitable share of the funds available, and if the assets drop 20% in value, then transfers would follow suit. In this fashion, the scheme finances are effectively indifferent as to whether members choose to stay in the scheme or to transfer out of them.

The rule of thumb of a 20% market drop, leading to a 1% annual cut in pension increases, together with a starting point of funding for full inflation increases at around 3% per annum, gives an indication of the strength of the system to withstand adverse conditions

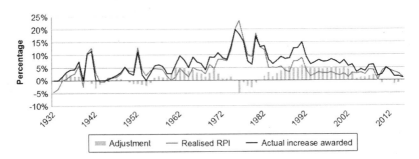

Figure 10.1    Historic Operation of a CDC Scheme.

before pensions would have to be cut. Back-testing of the Royal
Mail scheme design indicates that if the scheme had been started 80
years ago it would only have been necessary to cut benefits on one
occasion, as the economy recovered from the Great Depression (see
figure 10.1).

However, stochastic modelling for a scheme starting up today
shows a more challenging environment. Stochastic modelling
involves a series of many – typically between 500–5,000– simula-
tions or projections of future outcomes for the scheme. Within these
many possible outcomes there can be prolonged periods of unfavourable conditions that might lead to pension cuts. The potential
for pension cuts is an inevitable feature of CDC schemes, and it
would be misleading to argue that one can have all the upsides of
a scheme with none of the downsides. The question is whether the
frequency and severity of pension cuts is deemed to be acceptable,
and whether it can be explained to members. For the Royal Mail
scheme design, extensive proprietary modelling carried out shows
that over a prolonged period – taken as 30 years from the start of the
scheme – there is around a 20–30% chance of a benefit cut. So, we
need to face up to the reality of pension cuts and how these would be
communicated to members. There is also a non-trivial chance (of the
order of 5%) of what might be considered a severe cut, amounting to
a reduction of more than 5% of the pension. As a design principle,
we might want to consider some form of smoothing of cuts above

this 5% level over a short period of time of no more than three years. It would also be worthwhile to consider what will be happening to other types of pension arrangements during these difficult projection scenarios. In such a scenario, all schemes would come under pressure, although how the pressure impacts members may differ between conventional DB schemes, with higher potential for sponsor insolvency and a move to Pension Protection Fund benefits, and conventional individual DC schemes, with typically much lower member balances and incomes in retirement for those adopting drawdown solutions. Communication with members as and when needed will be key. When thinking about cuts in CDC pensions, we need to bear in mind that the likelihood of repeated multiannual cuts is vanishingly small, but the purchase of an annuity at the wrong moment locks in the reduced income permanently for the member.

Another example of where UK CDC will learn from others is in how they will deal with those limited occasions when cuts are required. Will trustees seek to soften the blow for pensioners, or will they, as has been strongly suggested in the consultation response from the Department for Work and Pensions (DWP)[5], treat all members equally with a uniform cut to benefits for active members, deferred members and pensioners alike? We know that in the Netherlands there has been an attempt to prioritise pensioners over active (younger) members, leading to resentment from the younger generation. UK CDC schemes will be required to publish their benefit adjustment rules in advance, with a strong hint from the DWP that uniform treatment would be preferred.

Another way of seeking to avoid delivering bad news could be to lean on the actuary to be more optimistic about future investment returns, and to thus paint a rosier financial picture than is justified. Preventing this has been addressed directly in the proposed UK CDC structure. All details of the scheme – in addition to the benefit adjustment rules outlined above – will be in the public domain, available via a publicly accessible website. Actuarial assumptions and factors will be open to full public scrutiny, with no hiding place for the CDC scheme actuary! When coupled with a requirement for a CDC scheme to go through an authorisation process similar to UK DC master trusts prior to operation and the extensive powers of intervention and direction by the Pensions Regulator, UK CDC schemes will arguably be among the most transparent and well governed schemes in the UK, or anywhere else in the world for that matter.

The DWP response to the UK CDC consultation sets out the benefits of CDC schemes, and points the way towards their wider adoption and use beyond the type of CDC scheme envisaged for the likes of Royal Mail. Specifically, this will involve a DB style set of target benefits for a single employer or multi-employer scheme, where there is no commercial angle or advantage to be dealt with. The DWP is quite measured, but accurate, in its assessment of the potential advantages of CDC schemes over the DC options now available in the UK market, in promoting:

• Potentially greater economies of scale than individual DC (IDC). However, the DWP notes the rise of DC master trusts in the UK market, which deliver those economies of scale to many UK schemes. One has only to look at charges now borne by UK DC schemes. These are capped at 75 bps as an annual management charge deduced from plan assets, but more typically are 50 bps all in for master trusts, covering record keeping, member engagement and investment charges , which makes them among the most competitive in the world.

• Potentially higher investment returns compared with IDC because CDC schemes can collectively cover a longer time-frame than individual members' schemes, which typically take on less risk as they approach retirement. This means that a CDC scheme can invest in less liquid investments, harvesting illiquidity premia, in a way that IDC cannot, given the need for daily dealing and pricing. This long-term approach of harnessing large illiquid allocations (up to 40% of scheme assets ) has been central to the long-term outperformance of the large Australian DC and Canadian DB funds. The DWP notes that wider use of income drawdown by IDC scheme holders may reduce the differential over time, but it is still too early with the UK's freedom and choice agenda to gain any solid view of this.

- A savings (pre-retirement) and income in retirement (post-retirement) option within one package.
- A proposition that is attractive to people who are uncomfortable with making complex financial decisions at the point of retirement. There is no need for members to make investment choices or to decide which of the many ways to convert DC funds into an income stream. This is crucial in the UK freedom and choice context. Members have a huge range of conversion options, from taking their entire life savings in one go on retirement, all the way through to lifetime annuity purchases, with multiple drawdown options in between. The market has not yet evolved to offer a sensible and suitably packaged post retirement product that balances the multiple and conflicting needs of members in an easy and easy to understand format[6].
- Sharing of longevity risk between members and across generations.

These latter points indicate the potential for CDC to play a major role in the decumulation of individual DC accounts. A retirement income solution using CDC principles – let's call them Target Retirement Income Plans (TRIP) – could be a major new component within the options available to people post-retirement. CDC incomes could be significantly higher than the corresponding annuities because of the lack of guarantees and hence the greater investment freedom and higher anticipated investment returns. TRIPs could be the replacement for conventional annuities. Both products address the question of how to generate an income that pays out as long as someone lives, which is one of the key issues facing DC members when adopting the income drawdown approach to spending their retirement pots.

However, TRIPs could feature more helpfully as a replacement for deferred annuities. Consider the blueprint for a retirement income suggested by the UK government second pillar fund pension scheme, the National Employment Savings Trust ("NEST"),

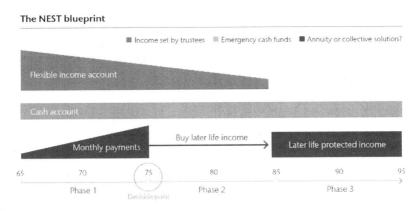

Figure 10.2   The National Employment Savings Trust (NEST).

illustrated in figure 10.2[7]. The use of a later-life protected income – that is, a deferred annuity or deferred TRIP – means that there is a finite period of time to operate the drawdown solution, a far simpler problem. But deferred annuities under the Solvency II insurance regime are very expensive[8]. This is not necessarily because the underlying product is expensive but because of the need to reserve against unlikely events. A one in 200-year event in longevity might mean a significant jump in life expectancy (for example, the discovery of a cure for cancer) and hence a massive increase in the value of a deferred annuity. Offering such a product under a CDC structure, where the members themselves provide any capital required, could lead to significantly cheaper TRIP solutions to combine with drawdown solutions, delivering the much-needed comprehensive post-retirement product.

TRIP solutions would pose further regulatory challenges. Dealing with adjustments and potential cuts would be even more crucial where the product is used to deliver an income on which the pensioner will depend. But if these products are sold commercially, it would become ever more important to ensure that the promised or indicated benefits are consistent with the underlying investment policy and benefit adjustment formula from the provider. There is no competitive advantage for an individual employer sponsoring a CDC scheme to oversell the benefits, although there could be for a commercial provider of TRIP solutions. The regulatory challenge is considerably greater to ensure that there is no detriment to the consumer. The number of responses to the DWP consultation show there is strong interest in further CDC options and developments[9]. The DWP note that they were *"extremely heartened by the number of responses arguing the legislation should be widened to provide for other CDC models, including multi-employer schemes, mutuals, commercial Master Trusts, decumulation-only vehicles"*. However, the department also identifies the need to develop the legislation progressively and to concentrate where the greatest immediate need is, indicating that they will initially focus on delivering a Royal Mail-type solution as the first stage of the roll-out of CDC in the UK.

## NOTES

1. McClymont, G. and Tarrant, A. (2016) "Towards a new pensions settlement", Volume 1, p.11.

2. Ibid, p.16.

3. DWP (2018) Consultation Outcome. Delivering Collective Defined Contribution Schemes.

4. Meeting guarantees require low risk investments for which the price is higher.

5. Op. cit.

6. This issue is discussed in depth in the Aon paper entitled The Future of (At) Retirement, available at: http://www.aon.com/getmedia/f50403e d-fba7-4f4d-9bd0-ff2b9103080f/Aon-The-Future-of-At-Retirement-whi tepaper.aspx.

7. Ibid, p.11. NEST's findings on the future of retirement can be found at www.nestpensions.org.uk

8. The Solvency II Directive (2009/138/EC) is a Directive in European Union law that codifies and harmonises the EU insurance regulation. Primarily this concerns the amount of capital that EU insurance companies must hold to reduce the risk of insolvency.

9. DWP (2018) Consultation Outcome. Delivering Collective Defined Contribution Schemes. Annex A.

# CONCLUSION

## Gregg McClymont, Andy Tarrant and Tim Gosling

When the UK government ended the quasi compulsory requirement to purchase DC pension annuities in the 2014 Budget, it transformed the way individuals secured their retirement incomes. Quickly, the outlines of the public policy challenge became clear: how to combine choices at retirement with the security of a reliable income for life?

Increasingly there is a difference in guiding philosophy between those in the UK who emphasise the word "pension" in DC pensions and those who see them as just another long-term savings vehicle. The former see the role of the provider as to help the scheme member save for retirement and receive an income in retirement. The second group see the role of the provider limited to help the scheme member build up their pension pot, prior to offering a series of facilitated choices at retirement between different competing retirement income products and cash. The first group is deeply sceptical about the efficiency of pensions markets given vast information asymmetries and well-established behavioural biases. In their view, trustees should instead act as surrogate customers and guarantor of value for money on behalf of most employees. The second group see all savers as active consumers in a competitive marketplace. These are fundamentally different visions and it is not yet clear which one will win out in the UK.

The UK has seen a sharp increase since 2015 in sales of flexible drawdown. The regulator of retail pension arrangements in the UK – the FCA – has identified that drawdown products are often expensive and poorly understood by their buyers. The FCA retains the option to introduce a charge cap if matters do not improve in terms of charging transparency (there is a 75 bp price cap for DC workplace schemes in the accumulation phase but no cap on decumulation product charges) and is promoting retirement investment pathways which try to make the complex options retirees now confront, easier to compare.

The FCA's regulatory philosophy is in the "market" camp, (indeed it is mandated as such by government). As such, the FCA continues to place faith in information 'remedies'. This is despite its own consumer research consistently finding them to be ineffective in driving more efficient pensions markets[1]. The research that accompanies the FCA's proposed retirement investment pathways is no different. The majority of people according to the FCA are unable to use the investment pathway information to correctly match the optimal asset investment allocation to their stated personal objectives[2].

In this context, it seems improbable that the majority of consumers will deploy the FCA's intended comparability tool to obtain services at the lowest price. It's highly likely in the face of complexity that most will default or 'roll over' into whatever product the provider with whom they saved offers as the eventual default. Furthermore, The FCA is not intending to set any parameters for the default products (for customers who do not make a decision), other than that the default cannot be into a product investing only in cash. Nor will retail providers be required to provide pathways with combined objectives, although they can offer them voluntarily.

This is where the new mass workplace multi-employer schemes – master trusts - which have emerged with auto-enrolment in the UK, should make their mark and persuade employers they will offer something that is in the long term interests of the companies' workers. They should have the opportunity under the trust based regulator – TPR – to build 'whole of life' pensions solutions that combine accumulation, income drawdown, a liquid 'rapid cash' account, and a later life annuity. The annuities will be bulk-bought from the wider market and the best wholesale price passed on to members, thereby mimicking what Chile has introduced on a national basis. The trust law governance requirements which applies to these providers means that if they have a default or near default then it must be designed to be in the best interests of their members.

The merit of the annuity element of the retirement product is that it ensures that members have longevity protection and cannot run out of income from their DC savings in later life. This is potentially much more important in the UK, where the state pension pre-tax is worth 22% of the average wage (and 29% post tax), compared to say Germany, where the state pension is worth 38% (and 50.5% post-tax)[3].

Most people will not have a diversified set of investments and will need protection against market vicissitudes for a core element of their retirement income. The cost of a guarantee will be lowest if the individual pools the risk of living beyond the average age with other savers. In other words, the retirement product must at least protect against both investment risk and longevity risk.

## LESSONS FROM THE CHILEAN ANNUITY MARKET

The most common way of providing a guaranteed income in DC retirement is via an annuity. Purchasing such a product used to be mandatory for those considered to be mass market purchasers in the UK and who were retiring with a DC pension. Pension freedoms removed the obligation. Annuities had become unpopular in the UK. This was in large part because low interest rates reduced the income insurers could offer purchasers in exchange for their lump sum. It was also partly because the market offered lower rates to those savers who stayed with the vertically integrated pension schemes with whom they had also saved – and this group comprised most savers.

International comparative studies indicate that Chilean retirees get the best value for money when they purchase an annuity. Since 2002, Chile has broken the direct link between the pension scheme and the saver by requiring that annuity purchasers use a mandatory and neutral national brokerage system, *Sistema de Consultas y Ofertas de Montos de Pension* SA or SCOMP. It provides prospective annuitants with the best three annuity offers in ranked order. Chile has been able to harness the market to work in the annuitant's interest.

This contrasts to the UK's historic approach, which enabled vertically integrated for profit savings and annuity providers to make returns from the information asymmetries which exist in this market between sellers and buyers. The vast majority of UK annuitants continue to default, 'roll-over' to the annuity offered by the insurer with whom they have saved, even when it comprises poorer value. The Chilean national brokerage system also applies to drawdown.

## DANISH DRAWDOWN AND CONTRIBUTIONS

In Denmark, annuities refer to products which have guarantees and also lifelong income products which do not have guarantees. In the case of the latter, if the value of the underlying investments decline, then the 'annuity' income will fall until the value of the underlying investments recovers. The Danish product is unlike UK drawdown because it is not an individualised product. Members pool longevity risk and this is why it is considered an annuity. In the UK, we would now probably refer to such a product as collective DC. Danish 'collective DC' may or may not include risk-sharing across generations, depending on the scheme, but it would typically not be the case. If in the future CDC were to be more widely deployed in the UK, it would probably be as a Danish-style "annuity".

An important factor in average pension outcomes is contribution levels. UK automatic enrolment combined contributions from employer and employee are relatively low. The figures for the UK have recently risen to 8% of the relevant salary band. In Denmark, contributions typically started lower than in the UK, at less than 1% of salary and were incrementally raised. They are set in collective negotiations, and vary by sector – but are typically now around 12%, with two-thirds paid by the employer.

## MEMBER INTEREST AND SWISS GOVERNANCE

UK trust-based providers are legally obliged to put members' interests first. This is not the case for the UK's retail style contract-based providers. The latter are obliged to treat members' "fairly". This is an ambiguous term. The OFT's 2013 report into UK DC pension schemes identified the problem of conflicted interests and poor governance leading to poor outcomes. The OFT recommendation that policy should be used to promote "robust independent governance" eventually resulted in IGCs[4]. This model is a first attempt at delivering "robust independent governance" in the retail-style individual contract-based environment but the duties and powers of the body are well below those which apply to trustees. In Switzerland, as in many other countries, workplace pension schemes can only be run by trustees. Switzerland puts great emphasis on the separation of powers between the independent trustees and the executive functions of the pension scheme.

## SCALE EFFECTS AND THE CANADIAN EXPERIENCE

The vast majority of low and medium earners automatically enrolled into a workplace pension in the UK are in a DC scheme and the majority of those members are with a few larger providers. There is however a long tail of small, often individual company schemes.

TPR estimate that there are just over 36,000 DC schemes in total in the UK, and about 2,180 schemes with more than 12 members of which only 80 have more than 5,000[5].

There are scale benefits that accrue to pension schemes which lower costs and increase the returns to members' savings. Self-reporting by small schemes to TPR's annual surveys continue to demonstrate a struggle to provide adequate governance and to assess value for money[6]. The total costs at the administration layer do not rise much as extra members are added (e.g. the size and cost of operating the board of trustees and advisers to the board can poten-tially be fairly similar regardless of the size of the scheme), and as a consequence the cost per member drops as each additional person becomes a member. Indeed, there is no evidence of any real limit to the benefits of scale in this layer[7].

At the investment layer, scale enables pension schemes to negoti-ate more effectively with asset managers and to drive down the costs of the latter. In addition, scale allows pension schemes to take some investment services such as infrastructure investment in-house. The costs of doing so can be a third of what financial institutions would charge[8], and, diversification into this kind of less-liquid asset may increase returns to members' savings. A 2012 report to the deputy prime minister and minister of finances in Canada found that pen-sion schemes needed to have CAD50bn (€33bn) under management to operate most efficiently[9].

## CONCLUSION

Chile, Denmark, Switzerland, Canada. This is not a football world cup finals group but instead, are the nations that the UK might look to for inspiration as it seeks to a build a retirement income system which combines the flexibility that the 'pensions freedoms' reforms of 2015 introduced, with the security and stability of traditional pen-sions, such as an income for life. This is no easy task, to be sure. A lot will depend on how far the new mass multi-employer 'master trust' pensions funds rise to the challenge of providing 'whole of life' pension solutions combining accumulation with post retirement investment drawdown, a 'rapid cash' account, and a later life annuity. To do so demands that master trusts change their focus from simple accumulation of member assets until retirement; equally it demands imagination from UK policy makers, who have to decide what are the ends of pensions policy in the master trust space. This brings us back to where the book began: to the divide between two views of pensions: the institutional one in which trustees govern a fund on members behalf with the objective being to provide a steady income for life and the retail one, whereby pensions are merely another form of retail savings. The government will soon have to choose.

## NOTES

1. The FCA research estimated that switching would rise from 8% to 25%. FCA (2016) Implementing Information Prompts in the Annuity Market, p.26.

2. Report for the FCA by the Behavioural Insights Team (2019), Increasing Comprehension of Investment Pathways for Retirement, p.17.

3. Figures from OECD (2017) "Pensions at a glance", p.103 and 109.

4. OFT (2013) "Defined contribution workplace pension market study", p.167.

5. TPR (2018) DC trust: presentation of scheme return data 2017 – 2018.

6. www.thepensionsregulator.gov.uk/press/smaller-dc-schemes-struggle -to-demonstrate-they-provide-value-for-pension-savers.aspx

7. Bikker, J. (2013) "Is there an optimal pension fund size? A scale-economy analysis of administrative and investment costs."DNB Working paper 376.

8. Bikker, J. A., O. W. Steenbeek, and F. Torracchi (2012). The impact of scale, complexity, and service quality on the administrative costs of pension funds: A cross-country comparison. Journal of Risk and Insurance 79 (2), 477–514.

9. Ontario Ministry of Finance (2012) "Facilitating pooled Asset Management for Ontario's public-sector institutions." Paper from the Pension Investment Advisor to the Deputy Premier and the Minister of Finance.

# ABOUT THE AUTHORS

## EDITORS

**Gregg McClymont** is Director of policy and external affairs at B&CE Ltd., the provider of the People's Pension in the UK and is a specialist in global pension systems. Gregg was a UK Labour member of parliament (2010–2015) and shadow minister of State for Pensions (2011–2015). He is a visiting fellow at Nuffield College, Oxford.

**Andy Tarrant** studying at l'Ecole Nationale d'Administration in France and is a consultant on Brexit issues. Previously, he was Head of policy and government relations at the People's Pension in the UK. Prior to that he was senior parliamentary advisor to the shadow Europe and to the shadow Pension Minister, having held a range of senior private and public roles in the European telecommunications industry.

**Tim Gosling** is Head of pensions policy at the People's Pension in the UK. He was previously DC Policy Lead at the Pensions and Lifetime Savings Association. He has also held roles at NEST and the Institute of Public Policy Research.

## CONTRIBUTORS

**Christophe Albert** is a project manager at the Conseil d'orientation des retraites in France, whose mission is to provide general (financial and non-financial) information on the French pension system . He has a PhD in Economics. He previously worked for the French Social Security Department on retirement issues and for the retirement scheme for private sector employees.

**Keith Ambachtsheer** is co-founder of KPA Advisory Services and CEM Benchmarking Inc, globally recognised advisers to pension schemes. Recipient of many industry awards, he is Adjunct Professor of Finance, Rotman School of Management, University of Toronto and Director Emeritus of its International Centre for Pension Management. He is an advisor to the CFA Institute, the World Economic Forum, the Melbourne-Mercer Global Pension Index initiative, the Center for Retirement Initiatives at Georgetown University, the National Institute of Aging at Ryerson University, and the Tobacco-Free Finance initiative. He is the author of four books on pension management.

**Jonathan Callund** is Managing Director of Callund y Campania Ltda., Chile's oldest, specialist consulting firm in employee benefits and financial planning, advising local and multinational employers on their contingent programs of group insurance and financial planning. He has worked for AIG's Global Pension & Annuities Director, based in New York. He has also acted an international consultant on pension and insurance policy for the World Bank, IDB and other multilateral agencies, writing and speaking on the evolution of the pension and healthcare social market reform initiatives implemented in Chile in the 80s.

**Anne Lavigne** is the senior economist at the Conseil d'orientation des retraites in France. She has a PhD in economics and became tenured professor of economics at the University of Orléans (France) in

1993. Since 2000, her research has focused on pension systems. She joined the Conseil d'orientation des retraites in 2016.

**Benita von Lindeiner** is a pension fund consultant at the c-alm AG in Switzerland and has a background in alternative asset management. Her PhD, sponsored by the Swiss National Bank programme, focused on agency problems, investment behaviour and dividend taxation.

**Olympia Mavrokosta** is a member of the Legal Council of the Hellenic State and a PhD candidate in social security and occupational insurance law. She was legal advisor to the Ministry of Labour, Social Security Social Solidarity during the pensions reform and a Member of the Management Board of the Unified Social Security Institution of Greece (EFKA). Currently, she is a member of the Committee for the transposition of Directive (EU) 2016/2341 regarding occupational pension funds into Greek law.

**Ueli Mettler** is a pension fund consultant at the c-alm AG in Switzerland, a lecturer at the University of Lucerne (HSLU) and president of the Association of Swiss Investment Consultants for Pension Funds SWIC. He is the author of the Swiss asset management cost analysis that led to the introduction of far-reaching transparency and governance regulations into Swiss pension law.

**Torben Möger Pedersen** is CEO of PensionDanmark – one of the largest Danish occupational pension funds managing defined contribution pension plans based on collective agreements covering more than 740,000 blue-collar workers. Mr. Möger Pedersen holds a number of board and investment committee memberships including Arbejdernes Landsbank, University of Aalborg, Danish Insurance Association, Copenhagen Infrastructure Fund I, II, III Danish Climate Investment Fund, Danish SDG Investment Fund, Center for Pension Research (PeRCent) at Copenhagen Business School (CBS) and Danish Society for Business and Education.

**Michael Schütze** is managing director of Allianz Corporate Pension Advisors in Germany, a joint venture of Allianz S.E., Allianz Global Investors and Allianz Lebensversicherung, which focuses on developing occupational pension schemes and funding strategies for large corporate clients. He also heads the corporate business and pension advisory business of Allianz Global Investors. He has been a member of the asset management committee of the German Association for Occupational Pensions (Arbeitsgemeinschaft für betriebliche Altersvorsorge e.V., aba) since 2004 and is a member of the pension committee of the German association of investment funds (BVI).

**Steven Tanner** is actuary and principal of PT Dayamandiri Dharmakonsilindo, an actuarial consulting firm based in Jakarta, Indonesia. He has been Chairman of the Council of the Society of Actuaries of Indonesia (2015–2017), member of the Supervisory Board and Chairman of the Certification Committee of the Financial Institution Pension Funds in Indonesia. He has advised a number of governments on pension and social security reforms.

**Kevin Wesbroom** is an experienced UK pension consultant and qualified scheme actuary who has been involved with many different strands of pensions, investment and broader employee benefits. He established the Aon UK Defined Contribution team and was the inaugural UK lead for Global Risk Services, a fusion of actuarial and investment skills for DB schemes. He is one of the leading advocates for Collective Defined Contribution plans in the UK.